ॐ

परस्परोपग्रहो जीवानाम्

TĪRTHAṄKARĀSANA

A Work on Jaina Yoga

BLESSING

The body is a medium for Self-Realization. Mental health is based on a healthy body. If one's body stays healthy, his mind can be blissfully happy. To keep the body and mind healthy, one needs physical exercises. This is one reason that *sādhakas* seeking Self-Realization use *āsanas* in their spiritual practices. To give modern meaning to this accepted and ancient principle, Shantilalji Parakh has linked the Tīrthaṅkaras with appropriate *āsanas* and *mantra*s. He has brought this practice out into the open, for the general public to benefit from. Performing such *āsanas* and *mantra*s is worth following by each and every *sādhaka* pursuing Self-Realization.

Ācārya Ānand Ṛṣi Mahārāja (1900-1992)

Beloved Second Ācārya of *Vardhamāna Sthānakvāsi Jain Śrāvaka Saṅgh*

Adventure of Consciousness

3

- Analytical Ayurveda/ Dr. K A Latheef
- Upanisads and Edith Stein: *A Dialogue on Models of The Person*/ Thomas Marottipparayil
- Tīrthaṅkarāsana: *A Work on Jaina Yoga*/ Shantilal D. Parakh
- Aparokṣānubhūti: *The essence of Self Realization*/ Dr. Shrikrishna Deshmukh

Śrī Satgurunāthāya Namaḥ

Tīrthaṅkarāsana

SHANTILAL D. PARAKH

A Work on Jaina Yoga

"logassaujjayogare dhammatithyayarejine arihante
kitteissam chauvisampi kevali"

Edited and with a new introduction by
Dinesh S. Parakh

MOTILAL BANARSIDASS PUBLICATIONS

Tīrthaṅkarāsana/ Shantilal D. Parakh

First English Edition : Delhi, 2019

ISBN : 978 81 940111 18

<u>*Also available at*</u>

MOTILAL BANARSIDASS PUBLICATIONS
40 U.A. Bungalow Road, Jawahar Nagar, Delhi 110 007
1 B, J.S. Compound, Kennedy Bridge, Nana Chowk, Mumbai 400 007
203 Royapettah High Road, Mylapore, Chennai 600 004
49, 8th F Main III Block, Jayanagar, Bengaluru 560 011

MLBD Cataloguing-in-Publication Data
Tīrthaṅkarāsana: *A Work on Jaina Yoga*
by Shantilal D. Parakh
ISBN : 978 81 940111 18
I. Introdution II. Appendix III. Bibliography IV. Asanas

Published by
Motilal Banarsidass Publications
mlbdbooks@gmail.com
Printed by Replika Press Pvt. Ltd

Dedicated as an everlasting memorial to my respected Father

Śrīmān Dagaduramji Dhanrupji Parakh

Born: 1891 in Khopadi (Taluka Kopargaon, District Ahmednagar, Maharashtra)

Died: 6 August 1969 in Dahigaon (Bolka) (Taluka Kopargaon, District Ahmednagar, Maharashtra)

He kept a balanced mental state in happiness and in sorrow. He was kind to relatives as well as to strangers. With his blessing, I learned business sense, social skills, and religious devotion. His dreams for and belief in me made me successful in both studies and in life. I cannot ever repay his debt! Grateful for his kind memory, I offer this humble work for the benefit of wise readers.

AND

To my dear Mother, Śrīmatī Zumkabai Dagaduramji Parakh, who, though old and infirm, travelled to Vaijapur to witness the blessings offered by Ācārya Ānand Ṛṣi for the publication of this work. She passed away seven weeks later on the 28th of June 1978, giving me the impression that she waited to see the book published.

Bowing Three Times, I give HOMAGE to and INVOKE

"A SI Ā U SĀ"

The **A**rihantas, **S**iddhas, **Ā**cāryas, **U**pādhyāyas and **S**ādhus of all traditions

AND

Lord Mahāvīra, the final exponent of the Jaina Path of Purification in the current era. Even after 2500 years of Kali Yuga (Jain: *dukhmā*, the 5th Ara of Avasarpiṇī), his teachings are ever new, ever true, ever practical, and everlasting.

TABLE OF CONTENTS

Preface

Tīrthaṅkarāsana pays homage to the 24 Jaina Tīrthaṅkaras[1] of the present era. It is the fruit of many years of meditation and *sādhana*. Piercing the veil of darkness and ignorance that obscures Reality is most difficult. True guidance often feels perpetually out of reach. But as I sat in meditation during that time of my life, the images of the Tīrthaṅkaras began to come alive, one-by-one, and revealed their deeper esoteric meanings. I could see clearly the *lānchans* or symbols of each Tīrthaṅkara, and as I practiced certain *āsanas* of Haṭha Yoga, these *āsanas* became connected to each Tīrthaṅkara. What was in those symbols of the Tīrthaṅkaras? Were they only for the prescribed canonical purpose of differentiating each Tīrthaṅkara? Or was there some deeper, coded meaning? There must have been a very special reason why the Jaina *ganādharas*, *ācāryas*, and *upādhyāyas* created special symbols for all of the 24 Tīrthaṅkaras of the current *avasarpinī.*[2] These symbols assumed great importance to me because they shone a bright light on aspects of Haṭha and Raja Yoga and connected Yoga to Jainism in a concrete way. After spending a long time in deep meditation and pondering the meanings of the *lānchans*, their deeper meaning and the linkages to Haṭha yoga poses unmistakably began to emerge.

---

[1] Literally, "creators of the ford" (across the river of human suffering)

[2] The descending arc of the current era of time.

It is impious to even think of changing the perfect knowledge contained within Haṭha Yoga or to modify the omniscience of Jaina principles. Fortunately, there is no need. Jaina principles exist in Haṭha Yoga and yogic principles exist in Jainism. Indeed, there have been a number of notable treatises on yoga written by Jaina *ācāryas*, including those by Ācārya Bhadrabāhu and Ācārya Hemacandra. This humble work is only the latest attempt to connect these two great traditions and demonstrate their essential unity, with a particular focus on *āsana* and *mantra*.

Anything that you may find of value in this book is due to the blessings of elders and Divine beings; any deficiencies are mine alone for which I humbly ask your forgiveness. Please do not hesitate to contact me to share your experiences.

May this book help unite the followers of all Jaina traditions and the followers of other religious traditions. May right faith, right vision and right conduct lead to universal peace and harmony, without and within. This is my humble prayer.

Acknowledgements

I have been blessed by Divine beings and *sādhus* who supported this work, especially my personal guru Śrī Vasantamuniji whose blessings enabled me to travel to North America and embark on a lifetime of teaching yoga to and healing others. Ācārya Bhagavān Ānand Ṛṣi blessed my endeavours in writing this book. Upādhyāya Śrī Amar Muniji provided much encouragement to complete this project. Mālava Keśari Saubhāgya Muniji and his disciple Jīvan Muniji demonstrated for me incredible feats of yogic prowess and encouraged me to publish this work. Jīvan Muniji also instructed me in the use of the rare, secret, and powerful *mantras* presented in this work and gave me permission to make these *mantras* available to the public. Respected Citrabhānuji explained the deeper meaning behind some of the *lānchans.* Ācārya Suśīlakumārji is well-known for having taught how the Ṇamokāra Mantra interfaces with the parts of the human body; he provided important additional information about the *mantras* and *āsanas* in this book. Śrī Pravin Ṛṣiji, disciple of Śrī Ānand Ṛṣi, provided reference books and engaged me in many hours of discussion about the contents of this work. Sādhvis Pritisudhāji and Madhusmitāji and other *śraman sanghīya* monks also showed faith in my work and gave their blessings. I also give sincere thanks for all that I learned from Svāmi Rāmā, Yogi/Svāmi Bua, and Dr. Vasant Lad.

I give thanks to all of my family members, past and present, who have helped bring this work to fruition. In particular, my son Dinesh spent long hours and made tremendous efforts to help realize my dream of presenting this work in English. This book would not exist in its present form if not for him. Special thanks also to Joanne Johnson and Paul Petock for the photographs.

Introduction to the Second Edition

Yoga is a means of returning to the Divine and understanding the purpose of existence. India's great fortune has been to have had an unbroken tradition of yogic practice and transmission for thousands of years. Yet India has not one, but multiple yogic and tāntric traditions. Scholars debate the exact meaning of the word "yoga" in these different traditions and contexts. But putting aside arcane *rājasic* academic debates, all traditions can be said to be broadly and fundamentally the same in terms of the end goal: understanding the fundamental nature of Reality. One should not be confused or discouraged by the glorious diversity of the *nāma* and *rūpa* of these yogic traditions, beholden as they are on the earthly plane to *kāla-deśa-pātra* – the variances and vagaries of the time period, place and vessel of physical birth. When one observes with a *sāttvic* glance, one sees what is held in common by all traditions.

It has become rather trite to characterize the Indian religious traditions as 'one destination, many paths.' But the cliché is based on the reality that the flows of subtle energy that underpin the yogic/spiritual/mystical path cannot be exclusive to India or to any particular tradition. The exhortation of the Ṛg Veda, एकं सद्विप्रा बहुधा वदन्ति, *ekaṁ sadviprā bahudhā vadanti*[3] finds parallel

---

[3] It must be remembered that Jainas, according to strict doctrine, deny the authority of the Vedas; the phrase is only an example of the catholicity of the concept.

statements in the traditions of every religion, is borne out by human experience, and is understood on a level beyond words by the spiritual adept. It is the awakening, cultivation & direction of that primordial energy called *prāṇa* (or *ch'i*, *ki*, *pneuma*, *spiritus*, *rLung*, etc.)[4] and the final settling of that energy into Blissful Silence, leading to the transcendence of the small 'self' into the larger 'Self' and union with the Cosmos that is the polestar of the *sādhaka*.

It is not possible to fully understand or effectively practice Jainism or any other religion without beginning to understand the yogic and mystical underpinnings of all religion. Merely knowing is eventually revealed to be an exercise in the most fundamental futility and will lead to the most disheartening dead-ends. As opposed to merely knowing, understanding is direct perception by the soul. In fact, *āgama* (as in the Jaina *āgamas*) in Sanskrit can be defined as "intuitional knowledge born of direct soul perception." It can be posited that the Jaina *āgamas* are actual descriptions of yogic experiences; not dreamed-up theory, but a faithful recording of actual perception of Reality.

There is a place for theory. But theory can only start the ignition; practice propels the vehicle – literally embodied as the *sādhaka* – forward. This book is written to inspire and edify the sincere practitioner.

---

[4] Danaos, Kosta. Nei Kung. Rochester, VT: Inner Traditions, 2002. See some additional names for *prāṇa* at http://www.neoduddhism.org/chi-by-other-names-around-the-world.html.

∞ ∞ ∞

"The relationship between Yoga and Jainism not only can be found in the texts dating from antiquity and the medieval period, but persists in the daily life of practicing Jainas."[5]

Jainism, like Yoga, is fundamentally a means to go within. Jainism has been inextricably linked with Yoga from the earliest times and a number of works, both ancient and modern, have been dedicated to the intersection and commonality of Jainism and Yoga.[6] Tradition asserts "that Jaina Yoga and meditative practices originated from Ṛṣabhadeva" while the earliest historical evidence of yogic and meditative practices can be found in ancient canonical works such as the *Ācārāṅga*, *Sūtrakṛāṅga* and the *Ṛṣibhāṣita*.[7] Though often purposely concealed from the lay practitioner – and without speculating on the reasons thereof – modern Jainism is suffused with yogic (and tāntric) practices. Praiseworthy efforts such as the (relatively recent) development of *Prekṣā Dhyāna* represent an attempt to restore the centrality of yogic practice to Jainism as well as to provide a coherent, systematic, and effective means of daily practice.

To offer a modicum of evidence on the linkages between Yoga and Jainism, let us linger for a time on one of the most famous

---

[5] Christopher Key Chapple, "Contemporary expression of Yoga in Jainism," in Chapple ed., Yoga in Jainism. London: Routledge, 2016.

[6] See for example the latest survey in Chapple, ed., Yoga in Jainism, Routledge, 2015.

[7] Sagarmal Jain, "The historical development of the Jaina Yoga system and the impacts of other Yoga systems on Jaina Yoga," in Chapple ed. Yoga in Jainism.

works of Jaina Yoga: Ācārya Hemacandra's *Yogaśāstra*.[8] Ācārya Hemacandra was a 12th century Jaina monk, scholar, poet, and polymath, "noted as a prodigy by his contemporaries" and as the "all-knowing of the Kali Yuga."[9] His celebrated *Yogaśāstra* (YS) remains one of the pre-eminent expositions of Jaina Yoga, and a worthy summation of Jaina doctrine in general.

The YS is immediately recognizable as a 'standard' Jaina scripture, but with yogic principles and references interspersed throughout. The opening invocation in the first *śloka* of the book refers to Mahāvīra as *yogināthāya* or "Lord of Yogis." In *śloka* 4, Hemacandra asserts that he has written the work based on knowledge gathered from the ocean of scriptures, traditional knowledge acquired from teachers, and knowledge based on his own experience. This triumvirate of sources evidences the centrality and antiquity of yoga in Jainism, while foreshadowing his own experience as the linchpin of his argument. He immediately continues in *śloka*s 5 through 15 with colourful and emphatic gems on the importance and nature of yoga, some of which are reproduced below (emphasis and clarifications in the source material):

- "Just as a multitude of dark and dense clouds [vanish] due to a forceful wind, [the results of] even the most evil deeds obviously dissolve by [the power of] *yoga*." (YS 1.6)

---

[8] I rely here on the translation by Quarnstrom, Olle. The Yogaśāstra of Hemacandra. Cambridge: Harvard University Press, 2002.

[9] https://en.wikipedia.org/wiki/Hemachandra, current as of September 2018.

- "Just as a quick [burning] fire [reduces] a pile of firewood [into ashes] within a moment, [the practice of] *yoga* destroys [instantaneously the results of] evil deeds although accumulated over a long time." (YS 1.7)
- "Let the man whose ears have not been pierced by the needle of the syllables *yoga*, and whose life is [thus] worthless, be deprived of birth as a man!" (YS 1.14)
- "Liberation is the foremost among the four goals [of human objectives (*puruṣārtha*)], the means of which is *yoga*. This [*yoga* which is also designated] the three jewels (*ratnatraya*) consists of [correct] knowledge, faith and conduct." (YS 1.15)

The references continue throughout the work. Various classical yogic *āsanas* are described in Chapter 4, from *śloka* 124 onwards. A detailed exposition of various forms of *prāṇāyāma* and esoteric physiology is given in Chapter 5. The YS also contains detailed descriptions of *mantras*, *jyotiṣa* and other divinatory techniques, various signs of impending death, etc.

While in no way discounting the value of the entire work, it is Hemacandra's own experiences in Yoga as described in Chapter 12 that speak most directly and memorably to the reader. The great Ācārya begins the section in no uncertain terms: "I have here [in the preceding chapters] faithfully expounded that which was obtained [by me] from the ocean of scriptures [and] from the mouth of my teacher. In the following [and last chapter] the pure reality proved [to me] by [my own] experience will be described" (YS 12.1). He then goes on to describe, in poetic and powerful language, the fruits of his experiences following the yogic path.

Hemacandra's faithful adherence to the rules of Indian scriptural exegesis, particularly *upakramopasaṁhāraikya*[10] and *abhyāsa*,[11] support the centrality of yoga in the YS. Yoga is mentioned first, mentioned last, and repeated throughout. The *Yogaśāstra* is a rich and comprehensive work, which the reader is encouraged to study (along with other works on Jaina yoga) for him/herself, preferably with reference to the original *śloka*s if linguistic ability permits. But I will hazard an attempt to briefly summarize what we discover in Hemacandra's Yogaśāstra: Hemacandra is deeply respectful of his tradition and teachers; Yoga is an integral part of Jain scriptures and teachings; the "pure reality" of yogic experience is something that can be obtained through guidance and practice; and there is no conflict between the essential doctrines of Yoga and those of Jainism. Hemacandra's Yogaśāstra leaves little doubt that Jainism and what he defines as Yoga, if not exactly equivalent, are inextricably and intimately linked.

Widening our scope beyond the YS, we find that many principles and points of Jaina doctrine find direct yogic equivalents. The foundational Jaina *Pañcamahāvratas* ('five great vows' of the Jaina renunciate, modified to *anuvratas* or 'little vows' for the householder) are exactly equivalent to the five *yamas* (restraints on unethical/immoral conduct) of Patanjali's Yoga:

---

[10] "Interpretation of passages consistent with the context of the themes presented in the beginning and end of a topic," as explained by Jyotiṣa master Hart DeFouw. Essentially, this means that topics at the beginning or end of a work are to be given elevated importance.

[11] "Value and importance of a principle is directly proportionate to its emphasis through the device of repetition," as explained by Jyotiṣa master Hart DeFouw.

JAINISM – PAÑCAMAHĀVRATAS	YOGA – YAMAS
Ahiṁsa	Ahiṁsa
Satya	Satya
Asteya	Asteya
Braḥmacārya	Braḥmacārya
Aparigraha	Aparigraha

Indeed, the observance of *yama* on a limited scale are the *anuvrats* while complete observance of *yama* are the *mahāvratas*. This equivalance should startle an astute reader with one of its implications: without diminishing them in any way, the great vows of Jainism are but the *very first step* on the eightfold path of Yoga.

Here is another example. It is well known that Jainism enjoins the avoidance of onions and garlic. What is less commonly known are the layers of ever-more esoteric reasons that the Jains are not to consume onions and garlic. The primary reason given by the monks to the average layperson relates to the amount of *hiṁsa* or violence done by uprooting and consuming these vegetables, killing the entire plant and destroying the multifarious and invisible beings contained within. A deeper reason to avoid these foodstuffs, however, is that adhering to this dietary rule cultivates discipline in the *sādhaka*, discipline being a *sine qua non* of the spiritual path. A yet deeper – and possibly the most important – reason is that onions and garlic can, on a subtle energetic and vibratory level, have a deleterious effect on the efforts of the *sādhaka* to enter into and remain in deep meditation, particularly at more advanced stages. This is also why onions and garlic are proscribed by not only the vast majority of Hindu and Hindu-derivative yogic traditions, but by any path stressing contemplation and meditation including Buddhism & Taoism. Though the two deeper meanings may be of limited interest and relevance to the vast majority of Jains, adhering to such dietary rules (and the rules of conduct more generally), both on their own and through the discipline engendered, purifies the vessel of the body so that when the subtle energy starts to flow, it can be contained safely and productively. There is a reason that *yama* and *niyama* (positive ethical/moral obligations) both based in personal discipline, come first in the eight steps of yoga.

Another example from Hemacandra, chosen literally at random, again demonstrates the esoteric yogic underpinnings of Jaina doctrine: in Chapter 3, *śloka* 60, Hemacandra states that "[According to Āyurveda], when the light from the sun vanishes, the heart lotus and the navel lotus contract. One should, therefore, not eat at night. [Another reason is that, due to the absence of light], one may consume tiny creatures." Provided, almost as an afterthought, is the standard "Jaina" reason for not eating at night (the possibility of killing many sentient beings) but only after the (more important) esoteric yogic meaning involving the subtle energy centres (*cakras*).

With these examples from the YS in mind, and remembering that Hemacandra's Yogaśāstra is but one scripture from an entire canon of Jaina works on yoga, one can postulate that Jainism broadly fits into the yogic tradition or that yoga fits broadly into the Jaina tradition; there is dissonance here only for those who wish to see dissonance. This yogic tradition is not 'Hindu' in origin but has manifested uniquely in the Indian subcontinent and taken on multifarious forms. Yet modern Jainism, particularly of the past few hundred years, has de-emphasized the yogic aspects, or dare I say, basis of Jainism. The effect has been to have at least partly severed Jainism from its yogic foundations, leading to no end of trouble and confusion as the *kāla-cakra* continues its descent into darkness.[12]

∞ ∞ ∞

The actual *nāma* and *rūpa* of ancient Hindu and Jain personages have many equivalents. Śiva is also referred to as Ādinātha (the first Nātha), and Ādinātha happens to be a synonym for the first Tīrthaṅkara, Ṛṣabhadeva. Were Śiva and Ṛṣabhadeva the same person? Perhaps. Does it matter? Probably not. Were Mahavīra and Buddha, whose blessed footsteps graced the same areas of the Gangetic plain at the same time in history, preaching a very similar doctrine, actually the same person? Perhaps. Does it matter? Probably not. The reason that it matters little, is that these historical or legendary personages are also archetypes representing eternal truth. One is clothed in Hindu (or Buddhist) raiment, the other in the garb of the Jains. Knowledge is Divine and ever-present. We tap into it in different ways and at different times and shroud it with the veil of meaning that best speaks to our individual personalities. It may be seen as sacrilege by some, but could it be that the actual individuality of the 24 Tīrthaṅkaras of this era are not important? That it does not really matter if they were historical figures or not? Might it be more productive

---

[12] Here is one notable parallel with Christianity. Significant evidence exists that early Christian fathers believed in reincarnation but that any references to reincarnation were excised from the early faith through, among other modalities, the Council of Nicea. The entire universe of Christianity has had to suffer lacunae in logic ever since.

for the *sādhaka* to understand them as representations or manifestations of that universal energy described at the beginning of this introduction? And to believe that the various *āsanas* and *mantra*s described in this work are a means of cultivating and directing those flows of energy, in line with the focus of a particular Tīrthaṅkara, and also in line with the *karmas* of the *sādhaka*?

The actual life details of the Tīrthaṅkaras may be important in cultivating devotion, but are not important to actual yogic practice; hence, this work provides only cursory historical sketches. There is little in this book about the scholarly details of Jainism or the antiquity of Jainism or even the main principles of Jainism, as these are subjects that are covered in numerous excellent and worthy publications. This is rather a work of *applied Jainism*, based on the premise that the very essence of Jainism is yoga and meditation, through which practitioners can reach the Divine. The heart and original contribution of this work are the *āsanas* and *mantra*s, and their linkages with the Tīrthaṅkaras.

This book, in the spirit of *prekṣā dhyāna,* is another humble attempt to reconnect Jainism with its Yogic past. The purpose of this brief introduction is to offer some clues and inspiration, and whet the appetite of the reader to discover and understand for him/herself that Yoga and Jainism are, broadly, one and the same. The *sādhaka* must discover the appropriate path for him/herself; the millions of gods of the *sanātana* pantheon (including the 24 Tīrthaṅkaras) are but an anthropomorphization of the slightly individualized path awaiting each individual soul, a glorious and multifarious symphony of methodologies. These paths have been gifted to living beings by the Divine as a means to understand and cross the ocean of suffering. Ultimately, those millions of individualized rivulets and streams merge into a single mighty river; the delta of that river, the merging of the river into the ocean, is the merging of the individual soul into the larger Soul.

The *āsanas* and *mantras* in this book can deepen your understanding and practice of Jainism. Jainism is Yoga and Yoga is Jainism. Unless entered into with the appropriate intent, academic discussion or debate is pretty much useless until practical experience is achieved, and after practical experience is achieved, discussion or debate is usually only a distraction.

This is not a work of theory. Rather, it is a work of experience and perception. This is above all, a practical work. Do not just read this book. Do not believe the author's claims blindly. Practice the *āsanas*, chant the *mantra*s and enter into meditation, then progress into deeper and deeper states of meditation and awaken the *kuṇḍalinī śakti*. Experience for yourself. Without practice and without penance, spiritual attainment will always remain out of reach. As the nervous system is purified, *karma*s burned, and the nature of the Soul is revealed, you will experience the dawning of self-realization within you. From that purification arises all knowledge and all power. From that purification emerges dispassionate compassion and transcendence of the small 'self'.It gives me joy to have played a part in bringing this work of my beloved father, whom I consider to be my first guru, to a wider audience in English.

May the reader find inspiration and value in this work.

- Dinesh Shantilal Parakh, Vijayadaśamī 2018

INTRODUCTION TO THE FIRST EDITION

Jainism is one of the world's great humanistic religions and scientific philosophies. It asserts the equal opportunity and the equal right of every single living being in the universe to develop its spiritual powers to the fullest, to evolve from Soul to Super-Soul. The *arhat dharma* can be called a religion without knots. Jainism does not promote blind faith. The people who followed the teachings of the *arihaṅtas*, who meditated on the lessons they taught, are called *arhats*. They questioned the Vedas and did not adhere to the caste or class system, specifically rejecting the hierarchy of the Brahmins. They rejected the violence of *yajñas*. They believed that one was bound to the cycle of existence by *karma*; that only the individual *jīva* had the power to stop the influx of *karma*; and that only the individual *jīva* had the power to eliminate accumulated *karma*.

Yoga is one of the *ṣaḍa-darśanas* or six systems of philosophy of the Hindu tradition. But Jainism also has independent and ancient links with the yogic tradition. For example, Ṛṣabhadeva, the first Tīrthaṅkara, has been called the Lord of Yoga (Yogeśvara). He had mastered many yoga practices. The Jaina *ācāryas* have credited him with profound knowledge of yoga. Each of his 100 sons was an expert in *brahmavidyā* and nine of his sons were masters of *ātmavidyā*. His eldest son, Bharata, was a *māhāyogi* who had also been the first *chakravartin* or emperor of India.[13] The *Haṭhayoga Pradīpika*, a celebrated scripture of

[13] And indeed, the reason that India is called Bhāratavarṣa

Haṭha Yoga, mentions Ṛṣabhadeva as a great teacher of Haṭha Yoga.

Jaina Yoga is linked to other religions and philosophies of India. Gautama Buddha's meditation practice was said to have been based on the teachings of Lord Pārśvanātha, the 23rd Tīrthaṅkara, teacher of Mahāvīra's parents, and a proven historical figure. There is speculation that the great lineage of Nātha yogis, including such luminaries as Matsyendranātha and Gorakṣanātha, may have arisen from the Jaina tradition.

According to Ṛṣi Patañjali, the first step in the eightfold path of yoga is *yama*, which is exactly correlated with the Five Great Vows of Jainism. The *Samavayanga Sutra* details the 32 *niyamas,* which help the seeker attain *mokṣa. Dhārana*, *dhyāna,* and *samādhi* are all discussed under *manogupti* in the Jaina *āgamas*. Elements of *rāja yoga* such as *dhārana, dhyāna,* and *samādhi* are closely correlated with essential practices of Jainism including *sāmāyika, pratikramaṇa, kausagga, poṣada, dharma-dhyāna, śukla-dhyāna*, etc.

The third step of yoga, *āsana* (the main subject of this work), also figures prominently in Jain religious culture. Go to any Jain temple and you will find idols of the Tīrthaṅkaras in *padmāsana* (seated lotus) or *khaḍgāsana* (standing pose). The Tīrthaṅkaras engaged in austere penances and body mortification for many years in very complicated poses. The lifestyle of many *ācāryas, upādhyāyas, sādhus,* and *sādhvis* from all Jain traditions suggest that they not only engage in but have mastered many elements of Haṭha yoga. One simple example is the ability of many of these renunciates to sit with erect spines, in various seated *āsanas*, for long periods of time. Numerous Jaina scriptures such as the *Uttarādhyāyana Sutra* describe *āsanas* in considerable detail.

Despite all of the preceding, however, the importance of *āsanas* in the Jain tradition has generally been neglected, especially in modern times. The lack of physical fitness and dietary discipline in the Jaina community combined with diets catering to taste rather than to health, has also concerned me for many years. It is hoped that practicing the *āsanas* in this book will not only have a salubrious effect on the Jaina community but also remind Jains of the importance of *āsanas* to their spiritual life.

The *āsanas* should be practiced for at least 12 minutes (1/4 of a *sāmāyika* or *muhūrta*) prior to the 48-minute *sāmāyika*. Upon regular practice, many physical, emotional and mental afflictions will disappear. Any person in any walk of life can perform these *āsanas*, whether householders or renunciates. The positive results will become evident once one is committed to practice.

- Shantilal D. Parakh ('Shant'), Akṣaya Tṛtīya 1978
  (Translated, expanded, revised and edited:
  Vijayadaśamī, 2018)

Essential Preliminaries

A. General Guidelines for *Āsanas*

1. Poses[14] should be done in the morning, ideally around sunrise. Alternatively, poses may also be done in the evening, ideally around sunset.
2. Poses should be done at the same time every day.
3. Poses should be done after emptying the bladder & bowels.
4. It is more beneficial to do *āsanas* with an empty stomach (before, or at least 1.5-2 hours after meals).
5. These poses are meant for healthy persons. If you have any medical conditions, consult your principal health practitioner (physician, naturopath, *vaidya*, etc.) prior to doing *āsanas*.
6. During menstruation or pregnancy, women should avoid strenuous or difficult poses such as shoulderstand, headstand, plough, etc.
7. Practice *āsanas* in your comfort zone without rush or fear.
8. Insofar as possible, practice *āsanas* in a place with fresh air and natural light.
9. Use a blanket or yoga mat.
10. Wear comfortable, loose-fitting clothes.

---

[14] "Pose" is used interchangeably with *āsana*.

11. The place of practice should be clean, without germs, dust, dirt, and insects.
12. Initially, do each *āsana* for a short period of time, about 30-40 seconds. Slowly increase the time up to three minutes for each pose, except for very difficult poses.
13. Use coordinated breathing and concentrate on each pose.
14. When doing more difficult poses, be extremely careful and cautious. Divide harder *āsanas* into sections and learn them in stages.
15. For maximum benefit, your diet should be as *sāttvic* as possible – pure, simple, healthy, small portions, and avoiding most if not all animal products. Maintain a happy and relaxed attitude during meals. Chew your food thoroughly. Do not fill the stomach completely: ideal proportions should be one-third food, one-third liquid, and one-third air (keep empty).
16. Cultivate right knowledge, right faith, and right conduct – the three jewels that lead to liberation. Have pure thoughts, a pure lifestyle and pure aims in life. Have friends who do not have bad habits (pursue *satsaṅga* instead of *kusaṅga*). Keep a positive mental attitude.
17. Relax for 30-40 seconds after each pose and take a longer rest after the entire sequence of *āsanas*.
18. Difficulty of *āsanas* are marked by *svastikas*:[15]

---

[15] If you are not of or familiar with the Indic tradition, do not be alarmed by the use of the *svastika*. It was an ancient auspicious symbol before being co-opted and associated with evil in the 20th century. The symbol is used extensively to this day in Jainism, Buddhism, and Hinduism.

卐	Very Easy
卐卐	Easy
卐卐卐	Difficult
卐卐卐卐	Very difficult

Start your practice with the "very easy" and "easy" poses, then proceed to the harder poses as you gain proficiency and experience. "Very difficult" poses should only be attempted under expert guidance.

Benefits of *Āsanas*

1. *Āsanas* can make our bodies perfectly healthy and resistant to fatigue and strain.
2. *Āsanas* make it easier to do *prāṇāyāma* and *dhyāna*.
3. *Āsanas* can help to manifest the latent extraordinary spiritual powers (*siddhis* or *labdhis*) and can tremendously increase will power.
4. General benefits of yoga poses include reduction of stress and tension; body and organ cleansing; improvement in the function of endocrine and exocrine glands; increase in spinal strength and flexibility; muscle strengthening; better immunity; and emotional balance.

Poses & Counterposes

Yoga is all about balance. Each *āsana* normally has a counterpose done immediately afterwards. For example, a forward bend should ideally be followed by a backward bend, such as the cobra pose being followed by the plough pose. You will see references to this principle throughout this book.

B. Yoga & *Mantra*

Once the *sādhaka* is comfortable with an *āsana*, *mantra* can be added. *Āsanas* will be most effective when done in a state of concentration and accompanied by an associated *mantra*.

There are at least four *mantra*s given for each pose. The *sādhaka* may experiment with using different *mantras* with a particular *āsana*. If the opportunity exists, the *sādhaka* should ideally consult a spiritual guide or competent astrologer to determine which *mantra* is correct for him/her based on the reader's particular *karma*, constitution, attraction towards a particular *mantra* and ability (for example, degree of proficiency in *prāṇāyāma*). *Mantra*s can evoke Divine presences and have Divine powers, so do not misuse, abuse, or disrespect *mantras* or recite *mantras* in an impure state of mind or body (for example, *mantras* should never be said in a state of intoxication or after having consumed the flesh of animals).

The following are general principles for choosing and reciting the *mantras* (in the absence of a guide):

1. For each *āsana*, the *sādhaka* should try each of the given *mantras* four times. Whichever *mantra* appears to flow easily or the *sādhaka* feels an affinity towards may be used for practice.

2. The longer *mantras* are meant to be recited in one breath. If it is not possible to recite in one breath, choose a shorter *mantra* which can be recited in one breath.
3. Longer *mantras* should be ideally be chanted 27 times in a row (in one sitting).
4. Shorter *mantras* (normally the first two *mantras* given) should be chanted 108 times (one *mālā*). If chanting more than one *mālā* of the shorter *mantras*, this can be broken up into several sittings during the day.
5. You can chant the *mantras* out loud in the beginning. Gradually, move to a whisper and as you become more proficient and able to concentrate, you can start saying them mentally only.

You will also see numerous references to relieving affliction of or fortifying the planets in the sections on *mantras*. These references are related to *jyotiṣa*, which can very loosely be translated as Indian systems of divination. *Jyotiṣa* is called the "eye" of the Veda and is a *vedāṅga* or limb of the Vedas. There is an independent but related tradition of *jyotiṣa* in Jainism as well; indeed, there are established traditions of divination in all Eastern and Western religions. The planets do not cause but rather reflect human *karma*. A skilled *jyotiṣi* has the ability to read that which is normally unreadable (*ādṛṣta*). *Jyotiṣa* is a vast subject, far beyond the purview of this work. At this point, it would be beneficial for the reader to know that the *mantras* can work directly to mitigate difficult *karma* by operating specifically on those areas of *karma* indicated by the planets in a person's horoscope, or more generally as indicated in the "Benefits of *Mantra*s" section.

Some *mantras* can also be recited in exact reverse syllabic order to create, amplify or reverse an effect. For example, णं द्धासिमोण (*ṇaṁ ddhāsimoṇa*) is the inverse of णमो सिद्धाणं or (*ṇamo siddhanaṁ*). Reciting the entire *Ṇamokāra Mantra* in reverse syllabic order may free one from enslavement/imprisonment/ bondage, the influence of malefic ethereal beings, and relieve pressures and troubles from one's hierarchy at work. **Experiment with caution; expert guidance is advised.**

It is important to remember, however, and especially in case of any confusion or doubt about the *mantras* given here, that the Ṇamokāra Mahā Mantra is considered to be the ultimate *mantra* of Jainism, agreed upon by all sects and authorities. The various *mantras* given in this book are for particular *vidhis* and *sādhanas* but one can never go wrong by chanting the Ṇamokāra Mantra!

C. Diacritics

This book follows the standard IAST system of diacritic marks for all Indic terms except those that may be in common usage in English (such as karma, guru, yoga, etc.).

Indic terms are normally italicized, except for those that are most commonly known in English or when used as part of a proper title.

For the sake of clarity and identification, some *āsana* names do not necessarily follow the rules of Sanskrit *saṅdhi* (like Shantiāsana, Kunthuasana, Malliāsana, etc.).

Full diacritics have been retained in the *mantra*s to ensure precise pronunciation.

For invocations from the *Svayaṁbhu Stotra*, extra breaks have been inserted into the Sanskrit (following the *padavibhāgaḥ* in the translation by Goyal) to facilitate understanding and pronunciation by the *sādhaka*.

Disclaimer

This is a work based primarily in personal knowledge and experience. It is not meant to diagnose or prescribe treatment for any sort of illness or disease. The reader should consult a qualified medical practitioner should any questions or doubts arise as to the appropriateness of any of the practices. Neither the author nor editor are liable for any negative physical, mental or emotional effects that may arise as a result of reading or practicing the *āsanas* and *mantras* in this work.

Anything of value in this work springs from the inexhaustible fountain of Knowledge; any errors are ours alone.

न हि ज्ञानेन सदृशं पवित्रमिह विद्यते

nahi jñānena sadṛśaṁ pavitramiha vidyate

'There is nothing as purifying as knowledge.'

Bhagavadgītā 4:38

पढमं नाणं तओदया

paḍhamaṁ nāṇaṁ taodayā

'First comes knowledge, then compassion.'

Daśavaikālika Sutra 4:10

Ṛṣabhāsana

卐卐

Ṛṣabhadeva was the first Tīrthaṅkara of the present era. His father was Nābhirāja and his mother was Marudevī. Marudevī saw fourteen auspicious dreams during her pregnancy, the first of which was a dream about a bull. Added to the fact that the newborn baby had the sign of a bull on his chest, the infant was named Ṛṣabhakumara.[16] Ṛṣabhadeva's skin shone with a golden hue. He was born in Āyodhya.

Ṛṣabhadeva was the first and foremost king and the fountainhead of much of the arts and sciences. He instructed his subjects in political science, social science, ethics, economics; and he invented coinage, writing and agriculture. His eldest son Bharata became the first universal monarch, or *chakravartin*, of India.[17] The *Srimad Bhāgvata* calls him Yogeśvara, or Lord of the Yogis. The *Haṭhayoga Pradīpikā*, a famous treatise on Haṭha Yoga, also refers to Ṛṣabhadeva as a great teacher of Haṭha Yoga. Ṛṣabhadeva's place of *mokṣa* is the mountain of Aṣṭapada.[18] His

---

[16] *Vṛṣabha* means "bull" in Sanskrit; *ṛṣabha* is a cognate.

[17] The name of India, *Bhārata*, may be linked to this particular son of Ṛṣabhadeva.

[18] Aṣṭapada is considered a "lost tirth" and is placed somewhere in the Himalayas; and some say is equated with the famous Mount Kailāśa.

lānchan or symbol is the bull. Ṛṣabhadeva taught people how to farm using a bull and plough, so I equate *ṛṣabhāsana* with the *āsana* of *halāsana*.

Procedure

Lie on the back. Keeping the legs together, slowly raise them to reach the shoulderstand pose or *sarvañgāsana*. Bend backward and place the toes of both feet on the ground. Bring both arms overhead and touch the toes. Slowly increase the duration of the pose from one to three minutes. Raise the legs back up to shoulder stand, then slowly bring the legs down towards the floor. Rest for a minute.

Benefits of Pose

- Neck, shoulders and chest become toned and muscular
- Pain is relieved and reduced in the lower back and hip

- Body and stomach fat is reduced
- Intestines and colon become healthier and stronger
- Beneficial to the liver, stomach and spleen
- Improves function of thyroid, pineal and pituitary glands
- Reduces blood pressure

Mantras

1. ॐ नम: ऋषभदेवाय :: om namaḥ ṛṣabhadevāya
2. णमो उसभाणं :: ṇamo usabhāṇaṁ
3. ॐ ह्रीं श्रीं ऋषभदेवाय प्रभवे मम ग्रह शान्ति कुरु स्वाहा :: om hrīṃ śrīṃ ṛṣabhadevāya prabhave mama graha śāntī kuru kuru svāhā
4. ॐ ह्रीम् श्रीम् अर्हं श्रीं ऋषभदेवाय नमः :: om hrīm śrīm arhaṁ śrī ṛṣabhadevāya namaḥ

Benefits of *Mantras*

- Reduce or remove the fear of thieves and robbers (including modern manifestations such as computer hacking, identity theft, etc.)
- Lessen the effects of snake poison
- Reduce or remove the fear of animals with horns, sharp teeth, or sharp nails
- Get rid of troubles caused by ethereal beings including ghosts (*bhūta*), spirits, demons, *preta*, *piśāca*, *ḍākinī*, *rākṣasa*, and other ethereal beings

- Give protection from floods; fires; weapons; angry & fierce animals and insects, including those that transmit disease
- Alleviate affliction of and/or fortify Jupiter
- Lord Ṛṣabhadeva protects the head, face & brain

INVOCATION[19]

विहाय यः सागर-वारि-वाससं वधू-मिवेमां वसुधा-वधूं सतीम्

मुमुक्षु-रिक्ष्वाकु-कुलादि-रात्मवान् प्रभुः प्रवव्राज सहिष्णु-रच्युतः

vihāya yaḥ sāgara-vāri vāsasaṁ vadhū-mivemāṁ vasudhā-vadhūṁ satīm

mumukṣu-rikṣvāku-kulādi-rātmavān prabhuḥ pravavrāja sahiṣṇu-racyutaḥ

He was not at all involved in worldly attachments, was quite detached, the wisest and the noblest of all. Lord Ṛṣabha, who had the full control of all the senses, was fully competent and independent, tolerant to all impediments, infallible in the Ikṣavāku dynasty, desirous of attaining *mokṣa*, renounced his vast kingdom extending up to the ocean.

– Svayaṁbhu Stotra (3)

---

[19] All invocations are from Nagar, Shanti Lal. Glory of Jain Tīrthaṅkaras, New Delhi: Eastern Book Linkers, 2006 and Goyal, Devendra K. (tr). The Path to Enlightenment Svayambhu Stotra, New Delhi: Radiant Publishers, 2000. Minor edits to the English have been made to correct typographical errors and for the sake of grammar and clarity.

AJITĀSANA

卐

The second Tīrthaṅkara, Ajitanātha, was also born in Āyodhya. His father was Jitaśatru and his mother was Vijayadevī.

From the moment of Ajitanātha's conception, no enemy attacked Āyodhya and no enemy attempted to defeat King Jitaśatru; therefore, the child was named Ajitanātha, or 'he who has not been conquered'. On his foot was the symbol of an elephant. Ajitanātha had mastered Haṭha Yoga's elephant pose and he also performed *gajakaraṇi (elephant) kriyā*. So in Jaina yoga, I have equated *gajāsana* with *ajitāsana*.

One Buddhist Theragāthā is called Ajit-ther. It explains that 91 *kalpas* in the past, Ajitanātha was Pratyeka Buddha. The Māhābhārata compares Ajitanātha with Lord Śiva. This suggests that Ajitanātha was known and revered not only in the *śramaṇa* culture, but also in the Vedic and Buddhist cultures.

Lord Ajitanātha attained *mokṣa* at Sammed Śikharajī.

Procedure

Stand up straight on a mat or carpeted floor. Bend forward and place both arms on the floor. The arms and legs should be kept straight. Without bending the arms or legs, walk on the ground in imitation of an elephant. Make the arms move like the trunk of an elephant by clasping the hands together and moving them like an elephant's trunk. Imagine your body as a gentle but powerful elephant. You may also do this with a partner: the front person will use the arms and legs like the trunk and front feet of the elephant; the back person will hold onto the front person's hips and will be the body and back legs of the elephant.

Benefits of Pose

- Helps reduced abdominal fat and flatten the belly area
- Contributes to better digestion by strengthening the stomach, liver and intestines
- Stimulates peristalsis which may relieve constipation
- Improves tone for the arms, elbows, wrists, fingers, feet, legs, and hips
- Improves blood circulation in the hands and feet, thus reducing sweating, joint aches, numbness and tingling sensations

- Relieves problems with stomach, throat, nose and sinuses; may also help with colds, allergies, flu, acidity, and headaches

Gajakaraṇi Kriyā (Cleansing Procedure related to Ajitāsana)

Perform this *kriyā* first thing in the morning, once per week or as needed. Be sure to take the guidance of an experienced yoga/āyurveda practitioner.

After emptying the bowels but before eating breakfast, heat 3-4 glasses of water to lukewarm temperature and add ½ to 1 teaspoon of sea salt. Drink the water and wait for a few minutes. While waiting, you may perform *uḍḍiyāna baṇdha* to facilitate the cleansing. Then, standing near a sink, touch your finger to the uvula to induce vomiting. You may vomit a few times, removing most of the water along with impurities in the stomach, mucus, germs and acids which may also come out through the nose. Try to ensure that most of the water you drank is vomited back out. You will feel lighter and rejuvenated.

Mantras

1. ॐ नम: अजितनाथाय :: om namaḥ ajitanāthāya
2. णमो अजियाणं or णमो अईयाणं :: ṇamo ajiyānaṃ *or* ṇamo aiyāṇaṃ
3. ॐ ह्रीम् श्रीम् नम: अजितनाथाय प्रभवे मम ग्रह शांन्ति कुरु कुरु स्वाहा: :: om hrīm śrīm namaḥ ajitanāthāya prabhave mama graha śānti kuru kuru svāhā

4. ॐ ह्रीम् श्रीम् अर्हं श्रीं अजितनाथाय नमः :: om hrīm śrīm arham śrī ajitanāthāya namaḥ

Benefits of *Mantra*s

- Any one of the above *mantra*s will help in legal disputes related to country, town, king, government agents, and moneylenders; also helps in disputes related to the home, family, jewellery, and land
- Protect the body against injury from weapons and facilitate healing after surgery
- Alleviate affliction of and/or fortify the planet Jupiter
- Lord Ajitanātha protects the eyes

INVOCATION

येन प्रणीतं पृथु धर्म-तीर्थं ज्येष्ठं जनाः प्राप्य जयन्ति दुःखम्

गाग्ङं ह्रदं चन्दन-पक्ङ-शीतं गज-प्रवेका इव धर्म-तप्ताः

yena pranītaṃ pṛthu dharma-tīrthaṁ jyeṣṭham janāḥ prāpya jayanti duḥkham

gāṅgaṁ hṛdaṁ candana-paṅka-śītaṁ gaja-pravekā iva dharma-taptāḥ

By listening to the doctrines propounded by Ajitanātha, noble people easily overcome miseries in the same way that an elephant gets respite from the burning heat of the sun by plunging into the deep water of the river.

- Svayaṁbhu Stotra (9)

Saṁbhavāsana

卐卐卐

Saṁbhavanātha was born at Śrāvastī, near the present-day district of the same name. His father's name was Jitari and mother's name was Senādevī. At the time of Saṁbhavanātha's birth, many intractable problems of King Jitari were resolved. Tremendous prosperity in monetary wealth and agriculture also accompanied the divine birth. Thus, the infant was named "Saṁbhava", which can be translated as "possibilities".

Among the thousand names of Viṣnu and Śiva, one finds the names of several Jaina Tīrthaṅkaras, including Śreyāṁsanātha, Anantanātha, Dharmanātha, Shantinātha, and Saṁbhavanātha. Being models for men and gods, Vedic sages equated these Tīrthaṅkaras with Lord Viṣnu.

Lord Saṁbhavanātha engaged in many penances and Haṭha yoga poses. One of his signature poses was *vātāyanāsana* or the horse pose. As Saṁbhavanātha's symbol is the horse, I have equated *vātāyanāsana* with *saṁbhavāsana*.

Lord Saṁbhavanātha's *nirvāṇa* was at Sammed Śikharji.

Procedure

Standing straight, place the heel of the left foot in the right groin. Place both palms on the floor. Slowly and carefully, bend the left leg and bring the left knee to the floor. The right leg should bend a little. Place the right foot firmly on the floor. Place the right arm over the left arm, intertwine the arms, and put the palms together in *namaskāra mudra*. Raise the elbows towards the ceiling. Come out of the pose and repeat on the other side of the body (i.e., with right foot on left groin).

Benefits of Pose

- Reduces trouble with the feet, legs and arms
- Tones and strengthens arms, legs abdomen, hips and buttocks
- Improves circulation to the spine, hips, legs and arms
- Reduces low back, arm and leg pain
- Reduces pain in the knees and feet
- Improves mental concentration and makes the mind more blissful

Holding *aśvinī mudra* while in *saṁbhavāsana* may yield additional benefits.

Aśvinī Mudra

Contract the anal sphincter for about 5-10 seconds and then relax it fully; repeat. This *mudra* should not be confused with *mūla bandha*, which is a contraction of the perineum.

Benefits of Aśvinī Mudra

- Alleviates and reduces constipation, diarrhea, gases, hemorrhoids, and urinary tract infections
- Facilitates the flow of *prāṇa* into the central channel (*suṣumnā nāḍi*)
- Helps to control nocturnal emissions
- By performing *aśvinī mudra*, *mūla bandha* may happen spontaneously

Mantras

1. ॐ नमः संभवनाथाय :: om namaḥ saṁbhavanāthāya
2. णमो संभवाणं :: ṇamo saṁbhavāṇaṁ
3. ॐ ह्रीम् श्रींम् नमः संभवनाथाय प्रभवे मम ग्रह शान्ति कुरु कुरु स्वाहाः :: om hrīm śrīm namaḥ saṁbhavanāthāya prabhave mama graha śānti kuru kuru svāhā
4. ॐ ह्रीम् श्रींम् अर्हं श्रीं संभवनाथाय नमः :: om hrīm śrīm arham śrī saṁbhavanāthāya namaḥ

Benefits of *Mantras*

- These *mantras* bestow better food, water and shelter
- Increase happiness in the kingdom or nation as well as in the lives of sons, daughters, wife, husband & other family members
- Give added wealth, better yields in farms and gardens
- Generally increase happiness and health
- Open many unseen, dormant possibilities
- Lord Saṁbhavanātha protects the ears

INVOCATION

त्वं सम्भवः संभव-तर्ष-रोगैः संतप्य-मानस्य जनस्य लोके

आसी-रिहा-कस्मिक एव वैद्यो वैद्यो यथाऽनाथ-रुजां प्रशान्त्यै

tvaṁ sambhavaḥ saṁbhava-tarṣa-rogaiḥ saṁtapya-mānasya janasya loke

āsī-rihā-kasmika eva vaidyo vaidyo yathā'nātha-rujāṁ praśāntyai

O Lord Saṁbhava, you have brought happiness and peace to the world. You are a self-healer for the people of the world, who have been suffering from worldly pleasures, desires and passions. You are a selfless and benevolent physician for the poor and helpless people suffering from ailments.

- Svayaṁbhu Stotra (11)

Abhinaṅdanāsana

卐

Lord Abhinaṅdana was born in Āyodhya. His father was King Saṁvara and his mother was Siddhārthā. His place of *mokṣa* is Sammed Śikharji. Many auspicious omens were seen in the kingdom after his birth. The citizens of Āyodhya were overjoyed and celebrated his birth with many festivities. Seeing the people's joy, the King named his son Abhinaṅdana, which can be translated as praising/delighting. His *lānchan* or symbol is *kapi*, the monkey. Hanumānji has been called Kapiśvara, or lord of the monkeys. I have equated the classical *hanumānāsana* or *anjaneyāsana* with *abhinaṅdanāsana* for the Jains.

Procedure

Stand on the ground. Place the left foot 2-3 feet in front of the right foot. Keeping the right leg straight, bend the left leg slightly. Place both palms in *namaskāra mudra*, lift them overhead and bend backwards. The arms, whole back and right leg should form an arc. Breathe in and hold the pose for 10-15 seconds. Breathing out, straighten the back. Change the leg and repeat the process on the other side.

Variations of *hanumānāsana/abhinaṅdanāsana*

卐 Sit in *vajrāsana* (bent legs, buttocks on heels), then lift the right knee up and place bent right leg next to the left knee. Right foot should be flat on the floor. Interlock the fingers of both hands and place them on the bottom knee. Place both palms on the floor next to your body and change the leg position, bringing the right knee down to the floor, buttocks on the right heel. Raise the left foot up and place it flat on the ground next to the right knee.

卐卐 As you gain facility with this pose, keep the arms to the side and keep switching (right knee up then left knee up). Try to do it at least 10 times.

卐卐卐 Without using the arms, jump up and change the legs quickly. Try to do it at least 10 times. Be careful doing this (e.g., make sure your toenails don't get caught on the carpet, etc.)

Benefits of Pose

- Reduces body fat, increases muscle mass
- Increases flexibility of the spine
- Reduces belly and waist girth
- Improves quality of eyes and face
- Can reduce headaches
- Reduces pain in the legs, back and arms
- Makes walking and running more efficient

Benefits of Variations

- Help alleviate ankle and foot problems
- Keep knee and hip joints flexible and strong
- Strengthen lower back & lower abdominal organs like bladder, intestines & colon
- Improve heart & lung issues

*Mantra*s

1. ॐ नमः अभिनंदनाय :: om namaḥ abhinaṅdanāya
2. णमो अभिनंदनाणं :: ṇamo abhinaṅdanāṇaṁ
3. ॐ ह्रीम् श्रींम् नमः अभिनंदनाय प्रभवे मम ग्रह शान्ति कुरु क्रुरु स्वाहा: :: om hrīm śrīm namaḥ abhinaṅdanāya prabhave mama graha śānti kuru kuru svāhā
4. ॐ ह्रीम् श्रींम् अर्हं श्रीं अभिनंदनाय नमः :: om hrīm śrīm arhaṁ śrī abhinaṅdanāya namaḥ

Benefits of *Mantra*s

- Improve the health of everyone, including self, family members, neighbours and those in the community, town, state, country, etc.
- Help fulfil mundane wishes and desires such as birth of children, major purchases, etc.
- Lord Abhinaṅdanātha protects the nostrils and lungs

INVOCATION

गुणाभि-नन्दा-दभि-नन्दनो भवान् दयावधूं क्षांति-सखी-मशि-श्रियत्

समाधि-तन्त्रस्तदु-पोप-पत्तये द्वयेन नैर्ग्रन्थ्य-गुणेन चाऽयुजत्

guṇabhi-nandā-dabhi-nandano bhavān dayāvadhūṁ kṣāṅti-sakhī-maśi-śriyat

samādhi-tantrastadu-popa-pattaye dvayena nairgranthya-guṇena cā'yujat

O Lord, on account of an all-round increase in infinite knowledge and other qualities, you hold the name Abhinaṅdana, which is quite meaningful. Accompanied by the damsels of compassion and forgiveness, you performed *tapas* and in order to achieve the aim, you required the quality of complete detachment both internal as well as external.

- Svayaṁbhu Stotra (16)

SUMATIĀSANA

卐卐卐卐

Lord Sumatinātha was born in Kanchanpura, near Āyodhya. His father was King Megharatha and his mother was Sumaṅgalā. He was born on the eighth day of the bright half of Vaiśākha month. During her pregnancy, Sumaṅgalā's intelligence increased daily, and she began to help the king in his difficult tasks of governing. This is the reason that they named the newborn, *su-mati*, or "great intelligence." Lord Sumatinātha's symbol is the krauncha bird.[20] He practiced many difficult poses for many years, including *kraunchāsana* which I have therefore equated with *sumatiāsana*. Lord Sumatinātha's *nirvāṇa* was at Sammed Śikharji.

Procedure

Sit on the floor, knees in front, soles flat on the ground. Place the palms on the ground and rest the elbows on the knees. Lean forward and lift one foot off the floor, replace, and then lift the other foot. After you are comfortable with these movements, then carefully proceed to the next step. Lift both feet off of the ground, putting the body weight on the elbows and arms, with the palms flat on the floor. Balancing the body in this way, bend forward and touch the nose to the floor for 10-15 seconds. This pose is rather difficult and requires a high degree of control, so

---

[20] A type of crane. The word crane is etymologically derived from the Sanskrit, *kraunch*.

you need to be very careful. Before trying to touch the nose to the floor, practice touching the forehead to the floor, which will give added support to the body as you master the pose.

Note: Image depicts an advanced variation of *sumatiāsana* which starts in *padmāsana*. Please follow the description given before trying to attempt this variation.

Benefits of Pose

- Makes the arms, legs, shoulders and neck strong and flexible
- Reduces belly fat
- Reduces pain in the hips and lower back
- Improves concentration and meditation
- Benefits many bodily systems, including nervous, muscular, and endocrine
- Clears facial skin, rendering it luminous and glowing

Mantras

1. ॐ नमः सुमतिनाथाय :: om namaḥ sumatināthāya
2. णमो सुमईणं :: ṇamo sumaīṇaṁ
3. ॐ ह्लीम् श्रींम् णमो सुमतिनाथ प्रभवे मम ग्रह शान्ति कुरु कुरु स्वाहा :: om hrīm śrīm ṇamo sumatināthāya prabhave mama graha śānti kuru kuru svāhā
4. ॐ ह्लीम् श्रींम् अर्हं श्रीं सुमतिनाथाय :: om hrīm śrīm arhaṁ śrī sumatināthāya

Benefits of *Mantras*

- Elevate the mind and mood; encourages positive thinking
- Help resolve legal issues
- Help lost persons find their way (physically, like out of a forest, etc. but also metaphorically)
- Promote equanimity during difficult periods in life

- Alleviate affliction of and/or fortify Jupiter
- Lord Sumatinātha protects the lips and teeth

INVOCATION

अन्वर्थ-संज्ञः सुमति-र्मुनिस्त्वं स्वयं मतं येन सुयुक्ति-नीतम्

यतश्च शेषेषु मतेषु नास्ति सर्व-क्रिया-कारक तत्त्व-सिद्धिः

anvartha-saṁjña sumatir-munistvaṁ svayaṁ mataṁ yena suyukti-nītam

yataśca śeṣeṣu mateṣu nāsti sarva-kriyā-kāraka-tattva-siddhiḥ

O Lord, you possess a noble, sound and rational mind filled with wisdom; because of this, you are called Sumati. You are clearly the wisest and the noblest, possessing all knowledge. Based on sound logic and reasoning, you have adopted the precepts of the *tattvas* (fundamental substances) explaining the true nature of substances.

– Svayaṁbhu Stotra (21)

PADMĀSANA

卐卐

Lord Padmaprabha[21] was born at Kośāmbi. His father was King Śridhara and mother was Susīmā. He was born on the twelfth day of the dark half of the month of Kārtika and his perspiration had the fragrance of a lotus flower. During her pregnancy, the Queen had an urge to sleep on a bed made of lotus flowers. On the newborn's feet were clear symbols of the lotus flower. For these reasons, the infant was given the name Padmaprabha, *padma* meaning 'lotus'.

In yoga, *padmāsana* is one of the most well-known poses and may have been named after this Tīrthaṅkara. In Jain temples, Lord Padmaprabha and all of the other Tīrthaṅkaras are seated blissfully in *padmāsana*. Lord Padmaprabha's *nirvāṇa* was at Sammed Śikharji.

Procedure

Sit on the floor. Bend the left leg and place the left foot on the right thigh at the groin level. Then bend the right leg and place the right foot on the left thigh near the groin. Both soles of the feet should be turned upwards. Place the left palm on the right ankle and the right palm on top of the left palm. Both palms should face upwards. The head, neck and back should remain erect. Keeping the eyes slightly half-closed, gaze at the tip of the nose or the centre of the eyebrows. Sit motionless in *kayotsarga*

---

[21] Also known as Padmaprabhu

like a Tīrthaṅkara idol in a temple. If you find this pose difficult in the beginning, try sitting in a half-lotus pose (one foot above the thigh only) and alternate both legs to evenly develop leg/hip flexibility.

Benefits of Pose

- Improves and tones the nerves and blood vessels of the legs & feet
- Relieves gas and heartburn

- Improves flexibility of the spinal column, thereby alleviating lower back and hip issues
- Combining *padmāsana* with *uḍḍīyana baṅdha* improves digestion and reduces illnesses of the stomach & intestines
- While in *padmāsana*, bending forward and touching the head to the floor (thereby entering *yogamudra*) may improve difficult cases of constipation and help to thoroughly cleanse the bowels; on a higher level, it will start opening the lower *cakras*
- Once *padmāsana* is mastered, the practitioner can remain in reflective/meditative states (such as *sāmāyika* and *pratikramaṇa*) for longer periods of time; *padmāsana* is the pre-eminent pose for meditation

Mantras

1. ॐ नमः पद्मप्रभनाथाय :: om namaḥ padmaprabhanāthāya
2. णमो पद्माणं :: ṇamo padmāṇaṁ
3. ॐ ह्रीम् श्रींम् पद्मप्रभवे मम ग्रह शान्ति कुरु कुरु स्वाहा :: om hrīm śrīm ṇamo padmaprabhāve mama graha śānti kuru kuru svāhā
4. ॐ ह्रीम् श्रींम् अर्हं श्रीं पद्मप्रभवे नमः :: om hrīm śrīm arhaṁ śrī padmaprabhave namaḥ

Benefits of *Mantras*

- Increase the light and aura (subtle energy, *ojas*) of a person undertaking long fasts

- Can greatly boost the career of the *sādhaka*
- Alleviate affliction of and/or fortify Sun
- Lord Padmaprabha protects the jaw & teeth

INVOCATION

पद्मप्रभः पद्म-पलाश-लेश्यः पद्मा-लया-लिङ्गत-चारु-मूर्तिः

बभौ भवान् भव्य-पयो-रुहाणां पद्मा-कराणा-मिव पद्म-बन्धुः

padmaprabhaḥ padma-palāśa-leśyaḥ padmā-layā-liṅgata-cāru-mūrtiḥ

babhau bhavān bhavya-payo-ruhāṇāṁ padmā-karāṇā-miva padma-bandhuḥ

O Lord Padmaprabha, your body befits your name and has a red hue like the red lotus flower. Your body was in full embrace of Lakṣmī both internally as well as externally. You are absolutely pure internally and endowed with infinite knowledge, while on the outside, your body is unsullied, most beautiful, bearing all the auspicious signs and devoid of sweat. Your divine teachings open the heart lotus in noble beings, just as the sun helps the lotus flower to bloom.

- Svayaṁbhu Stotra (26)

SUPĀRŚVĀSANA

Lord Supārśvanātha was born in Vārāṇasi. His father was King Pratiṣṭha and mother was Queen Pṛthavī. He was born on the twelfth day of the bright half of the month of Jyeṣṭha. Lord Supārśvanātha's skin had a golden tint and on his feet were clear symbols of the *svastika*, considered to be one of the most auspicious symbols of *sāmudrika vidyā*. The 'su' prefix means, among other things, best or highest, and refer to Lord Supārśvanātha's superlative qualities. The *svastika* is also symbolic of all things auspicious in Jainism, Buddhism, and Hinduism. I have therefore equated Haṭha Yoga's *svastikāsana* with *supārśvāsana*. In Jaina yoga, *svastikāsana* is also called *mūlādhārāsana*. Idols of the Tīrthaṅkaras are very often depicted as being seated in *mūlādhārāsana*. Seals and images from the Indus Valley civilization also depict yogic figures seated in this pose.

Whether we call it *mūlādhārāsana*, *mūlāsana*, *svastikāsana*, or *supārśvāsana*, this particular pose is an aid to meditation and facilitates the achievement of a blissful state. Any sincere seeker who wants to realize the Self should practice this pose. *Supārśvāsana* removes metaphorical thorns and obstacles from your path.

Lord Supārśvanātha's *nirvāṇa* occurred on the seventh day of the dark half of the month of Bhādrapada. His *nirvāṇabhūmi* is at Sammed Śikharji.

Procedure

Sit cross-legged on the floor. Place the sole of the right foot in between the thigh and calf of the left leg. Bend the left leg and place the left foot under the right. Grab the toes of the left foot with the hand and pull the left foot between the right thigh and right lower leg. The toes of both feet should be fully hidden so that energy does not seep through these ten gates (the ten toes). The right leg stays on top. The head, neck and whole spine should be in a straight line. Place both palms in *jñānamudra* and rest the wrists on the knees, palms facing upwards.

Benefits of Pose

- Reduces fat from the legs, making the calves stronger and more muscular
- Stimulates brain and sinus reflexes, thereby improving memory and reducing headaches
- Reduces hip, back and neck pain
- Reduces or removes lethargy

*Mantra*s

1. ॐ नमः सुपार्श्वनाथाय :: om namaḥ supārśvanāthāya
2. णमो सुपासाणं :: ṇamo supāsāṇaṁ
3. ॐ ह्रीम् श्रींम् नमः सुपार्श्वनाथाय प्रभवे मम ग्रह शान्ति कुरु कुरु स्वाहा :: om hrīm śrīm namaḥ supārśvanāthāya prabhave mama graha śānti kuru kuru svāhā
4. ॐ ह्रीम् श्रींम् अर्हं श्रीं सुपार्श्वनाथाय नमः :: om hrīm śrīm arhaṁ śrī supārśvanāthāya namaḥ

Benefits of *Mantra*s

- Any of these mantras can bestow prosperity in all forms, reaching the highest aims of life
- Increase intelligence
- People respect you as if you were royalty
- Chant one of these *mantra*s the recommended number of times and go to sleep. When you awake, whatever question you had in your mind at the time of sleep will be clearly answered
- Lord Supārśvanātha protects the tongue and speech

INVOCATION

स्वास्थ्यं यदात्यन्तिक-मेष पुंसां स्वार्थो न भोगः परि-भंगु-रात्मा

तृषोऽनुषंगान् न च ताप-शान्ति-रितीदमाख्यद् भगवान् सुपार्श्वः

svāsthyaṁ yadātyantika-meṣa puṁsāṁ svārtho na bhogaḥ pari-bhaṅgu-rātmā

tṛṣo'nuṣaṁgān na ca tāpa-śānti-ritīdamākhayad bhagavān supārśvaḥ

Attaining indestructible tranquility by annihilating all deeds and getting absorbed in one's own true self is the aim of all living beings, not to gain worldly pleasures which do not last long. Continuous increase in passions and worldly desires provide no respite from internal or external miseries. Such doctrine was preached by the learned Supārśva.

- Svayaṁbhu Stotra (31)

Candrāsana

卐

Lord Candraprabha[22] was born in the city of Candrapuri. His father's name was Mahāsena and that of his mother was Lakṣamanā. During pregnancy, Queen Lakṣamanā wanted to enjoy the cool rays of the moon, and she fulfilled this desire by gazing upon the moon many times. The newborn child had a white complexion and an aura of cool white light, like the rays of the moon. Hence he was called Candraprabha. As his symbol is the crescent moon, I have named a crescent moon-like pose as *candrāsana* to symbolize the coolness and softness of Lord Candraprabha. Candraprabha's *nirvāṇabhūmi* is at Sammed Śikharji.

Procedure

Place both feet about 1-4 inches apart and stand straight. Place both hands together (*namaskāra mudra*) and raise the arms overhead. Breathing in slowly, bend the body to your right comfortably. Your body will be in the shape of a crescent moon. After 6-10 seconds, breathe out, stand straight and bring your arms to your side. Repeat this procedure on the left side. Do this pose 8-9 times on both sides.

---

[22] Also known as Candraprabhu

Tīrthaṅkarāsana

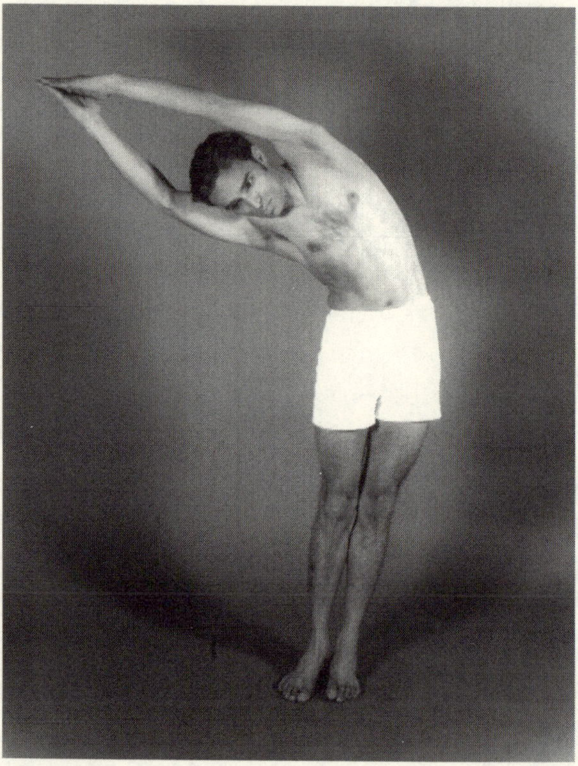

Benefits of Pose

- Muscles of the feet, legs, arms and back get stronger and healthier
- Reduces or removes knee and hip pain
- Calms pain in the sciatica nerve
- Increases back flexibility
- Reduces 'S'-curvature of the spine
- Improves digestion and reduces gases
- May increase height

Mantras

1. ॐ नमः चन्द्रप्रभाय :: om namaḥ candraprabhāya
2. णमो चन्दपहूणं :: ṇamo candapahūṇaṁ
3. ॐ ह्रीम् श्रीम् नमः चन्द्रप्रभवे मम ग्रह शान्ति कुरु कुरु स्वाहा :: om hrīm śrīm namaḥ candraprabhave mama graha śānti kuru kuru svāhā
4. ॐ ह्रीम् श्रीम् अर्हं श्रीं चन्द्रप्रभवे नमः :: om hrīm śrīm arhaṁ śrī candraprabhave namaḥ

Benefits of *Mantras*

- Exert a benefic influence on government officials, landlords, moneylenders, etc. to cause them to make decisions in your favour
- Endeavours with uncertain outcomes will have a positive resolution
- Alleviate affliction of and/or fortify the Moon
- Lord Candraprabha protects the brain

INVOCATION

चन्द्रप्रभं चन्द्र-मरीचि-गौरं चन्द्रं द्वितीयं जग-तीव कान्तम्

वन्देऽभिवन्द्यं महता-मृषीन्द्रं जिनं जित-स्वान्त-कषाय-बन्धम्

candraprabhaṁ candra-marīci-gauraṁ candraṁ dvitīyaṁ jaga-tīva kāntam

vande'bhivandyaṁ mahatā-mṛṣīndraṁ jinaṁ jita-svānta-kaṣāya-bandham

Lord Candraprabha had the fairest complexion. He resembles the moon itself in grace and beauty. He is supreme among the wise sages and destroys all the *karmic* enemies, evil thoughts, anger and passions. He is worshipped by Indra and other noble divine beings.

- Svayaṁbhu Stotra (36)

Suvidhiāsana

Lord Suvidhinātha was born in Kākandi Nagari. His father was King Sugrīva and his mother's name was Rāmādevī. During pregnancy, the Queen had a strong attraction towards flowers, so another name given to him was Puṣpadanta. His symbol is the crocodile so Haṭha Yoga's crocodile pose (*makarāsana*) is renamed here as *suvidhiāsana*. Suvidhinātha's *nirvāṇa* was at Sammed Śikharji.

Procedure

Lie on the stomach. Fold your arms so that the palms rest on each other and relax the whole body like a crocodile at rest. Now place the palms on the back of the neck with fingers interlocked. Inhale and lift the legs, folded arms and head off the ground. Only one part of the abdomen should touch the floor. Hold this pose for 10 to 15 seconds. Then, slowly breathing out, bring the head, legs and arms back down and allow the whole body to relax. Repeat at least three times; more repetitions are beneficial.

Variation #1 (卐): instead of lifting the body, place the palms on each other, place the head on the palms, and rest on the mat like a happy crocodile.

Variation #2 (卐卐): lie with the body straight, palms and feet on the floor. Walk forward with movement of the hands and feet.

Variation #3 (卐卐卐): in the same position, lift the hands and feet off the floor, hop off of the ground, and thrust forward about 10 times.

Benefits of Pose

- Tones the stomach and reduces belly fat
- Makes the whole body well-proportioned
- Improves digestion and relieves stomach ache
- Balances blood sugar
- Relieves constipation

- Improves appetite
- Reduces problems of the liver and spleen
- Reduces lethargy and revitalizes the body on a cellular level
- Reduces brain fatigue

Mantras

1. ॐ नमः सुविधिनाथाय :: om namaḥ suvidhināthāya
2. णमो सुविहिणं :: ṇamo suvihiṇaṁ
3. ॐ ह्रीम् श्रींम् अर्हं सुविधिनाथाय प्रभवे मम ग्रह शान्ति कुरु कुरु स्वाहा :: om hrīm śrīm namaḥ suvidhināthāya mama graha śānti kuru kuru svāhā
4. ॐ ह्रीम् श्रींम् अर्हं श्रीं सुविधिनाथाय नमः :: om hrīm śrīm arhaṁ śrī suvidhināthāya namaḥ

Benefits of *Mantras*

- Alleviate affliction of and/or fortify venus
- Increase power of discrimination to resolve issues with work, with the state/government, and within communities
- Lord Suvidhinātha protects the throat, thyroid, parathyroid and tonsils

INVOCATION

एकान्त-दृष्टि-प्रतिषेधि तत्त्वं प्रमाण-सिद्धं तद् अतत् स्वभावम्

त्वया प्रणीतं सुविधे! स्वधाम्ना नैतत्समा-लीढ-पदं त्वद्-अन्यैः

ekānta-dṛṣṭi-pratiṣedhi tattvaṁ pramāṇa-siddhaṁ tad-atat-svabhāvam

tvayā praṇītaṁ suvidhe! svadhāmnā naitatsamā-liḍha-padaṁ tvad-anyaiḥ

O Lord, with omniscient knowledge, you have defined the *tattvas* (fundamental substances) which disproves the ideology of the *ekāntavādins*. Your knowledge is based on tangible proof and makes abundantly clear the *tat* and *atat* nature of the substance. O Lord, no philosopher other than you could realize the true knowledge of the *tattvas*.

- Svayaṁbhu Stotra (41)

Śītalāsana

卐卐

Lord Śītalanātha was born in a town called Bhaddalapura. His father was King Dṛḍhāratha and the name of his mother was Nandādevī. His skin had a golden hue. After his birth, there was great peace in the kingdom. King Dṛḍhāratha had been sick with a painful fever for a long time. The pregnant Queen's touch reduced the fever and the king felt blissful coolness in his body. Thus, they called the newborn baby Śītalanātha (meaning the "cooling lord"). His *lānchan* is the *kalpa-vṛkṣa* tree (*śrīvatsa*) and his *nirvāṇabhūmi* is Sammed Śikharji.

After Lord Suvidhinātha's *nirvāṇa*, the *caturvidha saṅgha* of *sādhu-sādhvi-śrāvaka-śrāvikā* had fallen into lethargy and inertia. People stopped being compassionate and turned away from religion. *Sādhus* started to create and teach their own paths. *Mithyātva* was growing everywhere. In these sinful times, Lord Śītalanātha re-established the true meaning of yoga & *sādhana*. Like a strong tree, unswayed by the winds of falsehood, he remained true to the original teachings of the *arhats.* When we perform the yogic pose of *vṛkṣāsana*, our bodies channel the coolness of Lord Śītalanātha. Trees do not discriminate between good and bad persons or distinguish between humans and animals; they are dispassive and neutral, free from all *rāga* and *dveśa*. So for us, *vṛkṣāsana* equates to *śītalāsana*.

Procedure

Stand up straight. Bend the left leg and place the left foot high inside the right thigh; the left heel should be flat against the groin area. Keep the right leg straight. Intertwine the fingers of both hands and place the hands behind the neck. Your lower arms and elbows should be in a straight line. Breathe in and out deeply and hold the pose steady. The eyes should be focused on the tip of the nose or a spot on the wall. After practising for a few minutes, raise the arms overhead as you inhale. Raise your body up so that you are standing on the toes with heels on the ground. While breathing out, place the arms on the back of the neck and bring the heels down. If time permits, try this pose on the left side as well (otherwise, do it on the left side the next time you attempt the pose).

Benefits of Pose

- Improves circulation to the legs, arms and shoulders, thereby increasing their strength
- Improves mental concentration and memory, balances the right and left hemispheres of the brain
- Makes the spinal column and vertebrae stronger and more flexible
- Can help prevent osteoporosis
- Helps increase height in growing girls and boys

- To reduce inflammation of the sciatica: after finishing this pose, stand up straight. Lift the toes of the feet up and stand on the heels for a few seconds. Try to keep the right leg straight while lifting the heel of the left leg and keep the left leg straight while lifting the heel of the right leg

***Mantra*s**

1. ॐ नमः शीतलनाथाय :: om namaḥ śītalanāthāya
2. णमो शीयलाणं :: ṇamo śīyalāṇaṁ
3. ॐ ह्रीम् श्रीम् शीतलनाथाय प्रभवे मम ग्रह शान्ति कुरु कुरु स्वाहा :: om hrīm śrīm śītalanāthāya prabhave mama graha śānti kuru kuru svāhā
4. ॐ ह्रीम् श्रीम् अर्हं श्रीं शीतलनाथाय नमः :: om hrīm śrīm arhaṁ śrī śītalanāthāya namaḥ

Benefits of *Mantra*s

- Alleviate affliction of and/or fortify Jupiter
- Reduce fevers originating from imbalances of *vāta-pitta-kāpha*
- Reduce fevers of bacterial or viral origin
- Lord Śītalanātha protects the heart

INVOCATION

न शीतलाश् चन्दन-चन्द्र-रश्मयो न गाङ्ग-मम्भो न च हार-यष्टयः

यथा मुनस्तेऽनघ-वाक्य-रश्मयः शमाम्बु-गर्भाः शिशिरा विपश्चितम्

na śītalāś candana-candra-raśmayo na gāṅga-mambho na ca hāra-yaṣṭayaḥ

yathā munaste'nagha-vākya-raśmayaḥ śamāṅbu-garbhāḥ śiśirā vipaścitāṁ

O Lord Śītalanātha, the effect of the rays of your faultless words, mixed with the cool spray of your peaceful calmness affects the minds of the people of wisdom, who are well aware of the movement of the soul. These words are cooler and more comfortable than sandal paste, the cool water of the Gaṅgā or a pearl necklace all of which provide physical comfort whereas your soothing words provide mental solace.

- Svayaṁbhu Stotra (46)

Śreyāṁsāsana

卐卐

Lord Śreyāṁsanātha was born in Siṁhapurī. His father and mother were King and Queen Viṣnusena and Viṣnudevī. He was born on the 12th day of the dark half of the month of *Phālguna* and his *nirvāṇa* was on the 2nd day of the dark half of the month of *Śrāvaṇa* at Sammed Śikharji. While Viṣnudevī was pregnant, all the citizens of the kingdom became of noticeably improved character and religiosity; thus the prince was named Śreyāṁsakumara (*śreyāṁsa* meaning 'virtuous/righteous'). His *lānchan* is the rhinoceros. The rhinoceros often keeps its head bent down. While meditating on Lord Śreyāṁsanātha, I was led to perform *padmasarvaṅgāsana* (the lotus shoulderstand), which reminded me of a rhinoceros. So I equated this pose with *śreyāṁsāsana*.

Procedure

Lie on the ground or a yoga mat, facing upwards. Slowly raise both legs upwards until they are at a 90 degree angle to the body. Push the arms down to help lift the back straight off the ground. Now bend the arms and place the palms on the lower back. The whole weight of the body should be supported by the shoulders and the chin should touch the chest. Now fold the legs into the lotus pose.

The lotus pose can be assumed at any point which is convenient, including while initially seated or while initially lying down prior to rising up into *sarvaṅgāsana*.

When coming out of the pose, first release the legs out of the lotus pose. Bring the back down slowly to the floor. Then, controlling the descent of the legs, bring them also slowly to the ground. The total pose should take at least 1-3 minutes. Entering and exiting the pose very slowly increases its benefits manifold.

Note: it is advisable to perform the counterpose, *ārāsana/ matsyāsana* (refer to the 18th Tīrthaṅkara's pose) after completing this pose.

Benefits of Pose

- All systems of the body (circulatory, digestive, lymphatic, urinary, nervous, etc.) are rejuvenated
- Improves circulation to the entire body
- Reduces edema and fluid retention in the feet, ankles, legs and abdomen
- Relieves stomach issues, indigestion, lack of appetite, constipation, problems with the liver and spleen, excessive/frequent urination, sugar imbalances, etc.
- Improves circulation to the head/brain
- Relieves problems with tonsils, throat and coughs
- Reduces boils, hives, itching and skin problems
- Helps the thyroid, pineal, and pituitary glands
- Reduces bad dreams and improves quality of sleep

Mantras

1. ॐ नमः श्रेयांसनाथाय :: om namaḥ śreyāṁsanāthāya
2. णमो सिज्जंसाणं :: ṇamo sijjaṅsāṇaṁ
3. ॐ ह्रीम् श्रींम् नमः श्रेयांसनाथाय प्रभवे मम ग्रह शान्ति कुरु कुरु स्वाहा :: om hrīm śrīm namaḥ śreyāṁsanāthāya prabhave mama graha śānti kuru kuru svāhā
4. ॐ ह्रीम् श्रींम् अर्हं श्रीं श्रेयांसनाथाय नमः :: om hrīm śrīm arhaṁ śrī śreyāṁsanāthāya namaḥ

Benefits of *Mantras*

- Increase of all good things and *sukha* in the kingdom or nation (wealth, food, property, children, family, land and farms)
- Help improve the poor/bad behaviour of people
- Lord Śreyāṁsanātha protects both arms and shoulders

INVOCATION

एकान्त-दृष्टि-प्रतिषेध-सिद्धिर् न्यायेषुभि र्मोहरिपुं निरस्य

असि स्म कैवल्य-विभूति-सम्राट ततस्त्व-मर्हन् नसि में स्तवार्हः

ekānta-dṛṣṭa-pratiṣedha-siddhir nyāyeśubhir moharipuṁ nirasya

asi sma kaivalya vibhūti samrāṭa tatastva-marhan nasi meṁ stavārhaḥ

O Lord, the negation of the view of the *ekāntavādins*, is accomplished by using strong, forceful and judicious arguments. You have always been victorious over your opponents by your true and sound arguments. O Arhaṅta, you who have overpowered your enemies filled with ignorance and deluding *karmas*, have achieved the glory of *kevalajñāna*. You have thus become the lord of the majestic beauty of the *samvasaraṇa*. I humbly pray to you, offering my salutation.

- Svayaṁbhu Stotra (55)

VĀSUPŪJYĀSANA

卐

Lord Vāsupūjya was born in a town called Champapuri. His father was King Vasupūjya and his mother was Queen Jayādevī. He was the first Tīrthaṅkara who was not married and took *dikṣa* while celibate. His symbol is the buffalo and his *nirvāṇa* was at Sammed Śikharji.

When we practice the *āsana* called *gomukhāsana*, it opens our hearts to compassion for all living beings, including buffalos. By naming this *āsana* as *vāsupūjyāsana*, we are reminded of Vāsupūjya's teachings to honour and protect all living beings.

Procedure

Sitting on the ground, bend the left leg and place the left heel under the buttock. Bend the right leg and place over top of the left leg in such a way that both knees are on top of each other. Bend the left arm over the head with the left hand in between the shoulder blade. Bend the right arm behind the back and raise it up so that the fingers of both hands touch each other. Try to interlock the fingers of both hands. You can try reversing the position of the arms and legs, either in the same session or the next time you attempt the pose.

Tīrthaṅkarāsana

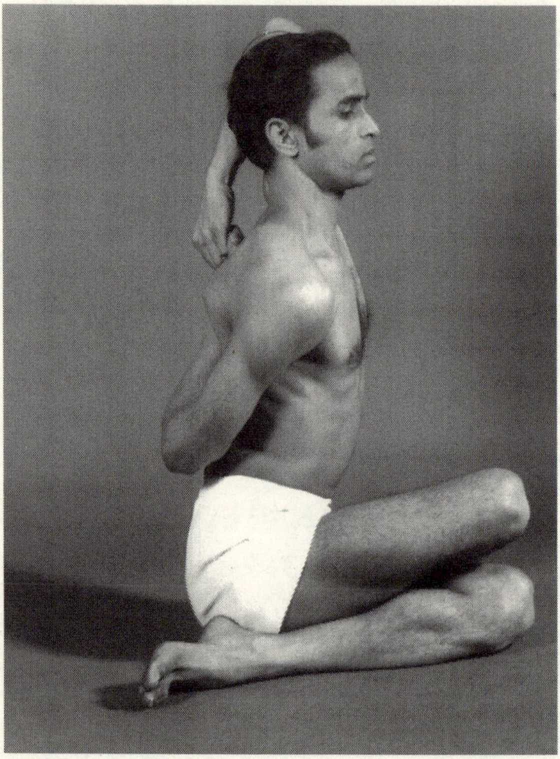

Benefits of Pose

- Vāsupūjya protects the arms and hands. In this *āsana*, the arrangement of the arms over and behind the back is very important and provides numerous benefits to the shoulders, elbows and wrists
- Strengthens and increases flexibility in the fingers, hands, arms, shoulders and chest
- Strengthens and tones the muscles of the legs

- Relieves reproductive and urinary tract complaints
- Benefits the ribs, back and waist
- Corrects the breathing
- Relieves gases and heartburn
- Variation: bending forward while in this pose helps to balance *kāpha-vāta-pitta doṣas*

Mantras

1. ॐ नमः वासुपूज्यनाथाय :: om namaḥ vāsupūjyanāthāya
2. णमो वासुपूज्याणं :: ṇamo vāsupujyaṇam
3. ॐ ह्रीम् श्रींम् णमो भगवते वासुपूज्य प्रभवे मम ग्रह शान्ति कुरु कुरु स्वाहा :: om hrīm śrīm ṇamo bhagavate vāsupūjya prabhave mama graha śānti kuru kuru svāhā
4. ॐ ह्रीम् श्रींम् अर्हं श्रीं वासुपूज्याय नमः :: om hrīm śrīm arhaṁ śrī vāsupūjyāya namaḥ

Benefits of *Mantras*

- Alleviate affliction of and/or fortify Mars
- Increase health and happiness for the *sādhaka* and people around him/her
- Improve the yield of farms and gardens
- Raise one's status in employment and government
- Relieve faults of *vāstu* in home, business, farms
- Protect against anger/displeasure from ethereal beings
- Lord Vāsupūjya protects both the hands and arms

INVOCATION

शिवासु पूज्योऽभ्यु-दय-क्रियासु त्वं वासुपूज्यस् त्रिदशेन्द्रपूज्यः

मयापि पूज्योऽल्प-धिया मुनीन्द्र दीपार्चिषा किं तपनो न पूज्यः

śīvāsu pūjyo'bhyu-daya-kriyāsu tvaṁ vāsupūjyas tridaśendra-pūjyaḥ

mayāpi pūjyo'lpa-dhiyā munīndra dīpārchiṣā kiṁ tapano na pūjyaḥ

O Lord of the sages and the *gaṇadharas*, known as Vāsupūjya, you are adored by all including Indra and the best of the *cakravartin* kings on all the auspicious occasions. You are also adored by me having little wisdom, just as the sun is adored by the small lamp.

- Svayaṁbhu Stotra (56)

Vimalāsana

卐卐卐

Lord Vimalanātha was born in Kampilpur. His father was King Kṛutavarmā and his mother was Queen Śyāmādevī. He was born on the 3rd day of the month of *Māgha*, *śukla pakṣa* (bright half) at midnight. During her pregnancy, Śyāmādevī felt a great cleansing of her mind and body. So the child was named Vimalanātha (*vimala* meaning 'spotless, without dirt'). Vimalanātha's *lānchan* is the boar and his *nirvāṇabhūmi* was Sammed Śikharji.

In olden days, people used to use the bow and arrow to kill large numbers of innocent animals. Out of compassion and detachment (*vairāgya*), Vimalanātha dropped his bow and arrow and prevailed upon others to do the same. The animals were now protected and safe because of this momentous gesture. Vimalanātha accepted monkhood with 1,000 other kings in a forest of mango trees.

The bow pose or *dhanurāsana* reminds us of Vimalanātha's great act of compassion towards animals. Vimalanātha protects the thumb and fingers of the hands. And without the thumb and fingers, one cannot use a bow and arrows. For these reasons, I have equated *vimalasāna* with *dhanurāsana*.

Procedure

Lie face down on the ground or a mat and let the arms, legs and body be totally relaxed. Bend the legs and arms and grab both ankles with both hands. Keep the feet close to each other. While inhaling, slowly lift the head off the floor, arch the back and lift the arms and legs towards the ceiling. Make sure you feel a nice pull on the spinal column. Breathe in and hold the pose for 10-15 seconds. While exhaling, release the ankles and bring the head and chest to the floor. Relax the whole body.

Variation: As you get more comfortable with this pose, you may roll to the right and left a few times while holding the pose.

Variation (advanced): While in *vimalāsana*, rock forward and backward at least 10 times.

Benefits of Pose

- Entire back and spinal column become stronger and more flexible
- Reduces abdominal fat
- Muscles and bones of the legs and arms get strengthened and toned
- Stimulates digestive secretions to improve digestion and elimination
- Tones the ribs, heart and lungs
- Women get extra cleansing benefit during menses; beneficial for ovaries and uterus; relieves pre-menstrual syndrome

Mantras

1. ॐ नमः विमलनाथाय :: om namaḥ vimalanāthāya
2. णमो विमलाणं :: ṇamo vimalāṇaṁ
3. ॐ ह्रीम् श्रींम् श्रीं विमलनाथाय प्रभवे मम ग्रह शान्ति कुरु कुरु स्वाहा :: om hrīm śrīm śrī vimalanāthāya prabhave mama graha śānti kuru kuru svāhā
4. ॐ ह्रीम् श्रींम् अर्हं श्रीं विमलनाथाय नमः :: om hrīm śrīm arhaṁ śrī vimalanāthāya namaḥ

Benefits of *Mantras*

- Help concentration and meditation practices, remove obstructions to knowledge, and quieten the mind
- Increase the *sādhaka*'s popularity and respect in the world

- Alleviate affliction to and/or fortify Mercury
- Lord Vimalanātha protects the fingers

INVOCATION

य एव नित्यक्षणिकादयो नया मिथोऽन-पेक्षाः स्व-पर-प्रणाशिनः

त एव तत्त्वं विमलस्य ते मुनेः परस्परेक्षाः स्व-परोप-कारिणः

ya eva nitya-kṣaṇikādayo nayā mitho’n-apekṣāḥ sva-para-praṇāśiṇaḥ

ta eva tatvaṁ vimalasya te muneḥ parasparekṣāḥ sva-paropa-kāriṇaḥ

O Lord, you are free of all the *karma*s and are competent to comprehend all the things fully and directly by yourself. Equipped with that quality, you have studied and analysed the *tattvas* (fundamental substances) from all angles and established their nature. Your teachings are most judicious and satisfying to all in every way.

- Svayaṁbhu Stotra (61)

Anantāsana

卐卐卐

Lord Anantanātha was born in Ayodhyā on the 3rd day of the dark half of *Vaiśākha* month and obtained *nirvāṇa* on the 5th day of the bright half of *Caitra* month at Sammed Śikharji. His father was King Siṁhasena and his mother was Queen Suyaśā. His *lānchan* is the hawk/eagle.

When Anantanātha attained *kevalajñāna*, everyone became happy in Āyodhya. Thousands of peacocks started singing and dancing in the mango orchards on this auspicious occasion. Therefore, the Haṭha Yoga pose of *mayurāsana* (peacock pose) can be considered equivalent to *anantāsana*.[23]

Procedure

Kneel on the ground or yoga mat sitting on the heels. Bring the elbows together and place the palms on the floor, with the fingers pointing towards the feet. Keep a comfortable distance between the palms. Place the elbows on the navel and put the body weight on the palms. Gently breathing in, push the body forward, ensuring that the elbows do not slide from the navel.

---

[23] Lord Anantanātha's symbol also associates the eagle pose (*garuḍāsana*) with *anantāsana*.

This manoeuvre will lift the feet above the ground without trying to force them up. In this pose, the head, torso and legs should be in a straight line parallel to the floor. Hold the pose for 8-10 seconds while retaining the breath. Upon exhalation, relax the body and let the toes touch the ground. Repeat the pose a few times, each time increasing the duration for which it is held (maximum hold time should be about 1 minute).

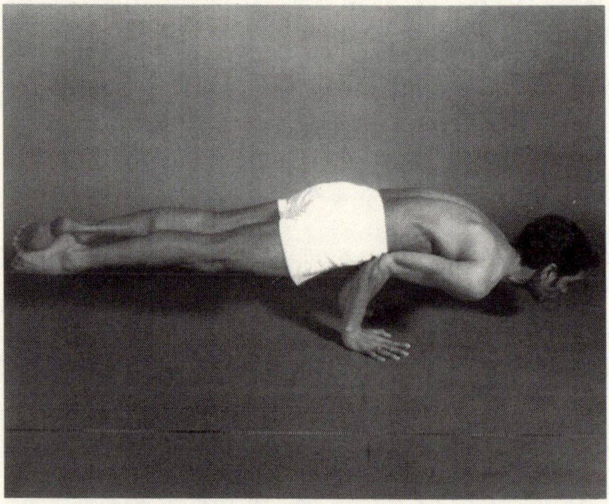

Variation: point the fingers forward

Variation: enter this pose from *padmāsana*

Benefits of Pose

- Benefits the digestive system
- Tones the abdominal organs such as the liver, pancreas, stomach and spleen
- Reduces gas (*vāta*) and acidity (*pitta*)

- Regular practice will prevent constipation, indigestion, diabetes and edema
- Strengthens wrists, elbows, forearms and abdomen

Mantras

1. ॐ नमः अनन्तनाथाय :: om namaḥ anantanāthāya
2. णमो अनन्ताणं :: ṇamo anantāṇaṁ
3. ॐ ह्रीम् श्रींम् नमः अनन्तनाथाय प्रभवे मम ग्रह शान्ति कुरु कुरु स्वाहा :: om hrīm śrīm namaḥ anantanāthāya prabhave mama graha śānti kuru kuru svāhā
4. ॐ ह्रीम् श्रींम् अर्हं श्रीं अनन्तनाथाय नमः :: om hrīm śrīm arhaṁ śrī anantanāthāya namaḥ

Benefits of *Mantras*

- Alleviate affliction to and/or fortify Mercury
- Bless the *sādhaka* with more healthful, higher quality and quantity of food; prosperity; and good children
- Advance the *sādhaka* to higher positions in career
- Bless the *sādhaka* with wisdom & deeper knowledge of many subjects
- Lord Anantanātha protects the nails and the delicate nerves underneath

INVOCATION

अनन्त-दोषा-शय-विग्रहो ग्रहो विषङ्ग-वान् मोह-मयश्चिरं हृयदि

यतो जितस्तत्त्व-रुचौ प्रसीदता त्वया ततोऽभू र्भगवा-ननन्त-जित्

ananta-doṣā-śaya-vigraho graho viṣaṅga-vān moha-mayaściraṁ hyadi

yato jitastattva-rucau prasīdatā tvayā tato'bhūrbhagavā-nananta-jit

You have conquered the demon of infatuation and illusion from time immemorial and as you have been happy with pursuing knowledge of the *tattvas* (fundamental substances), so, O Lord, your name as Anantanātha is fully justified.

- Svayaṁbhu Stotra (66)

Dharmāsana

The 15th Tīrthaṅkara, Lord Dharmanātha was born in Ratnapuri as the son of King Bhānurājā and Queen Suvratā. While pregnant, Suvratā had the urge to be even more ethical, moral and religious; hence the child was named Dharmanātha (lord of *dharma*). His symbol is the thunderbolt or *vajra*. To remind us of the exalted nature of Lord Dharmanātha, I equate Haṭha Yoga's *vajra-ṣīrśāsana* with *dharmāsana*.

In his first *deśnā* (religious discourse) after attaining *kevalajñāna*, Dharmanātha spoke of not worrying about outside enemies but rather to battle and conquer the inner enemies such as anger, ego, greed, etc., and that victory in this battle would lead to true happiness and perpetual peace.

Lord Dharmanātha's place of *nirvāṇa* is Sammed Śikharji.

Procedure

Carefully enter into the yogic headstand (*ṣīrśāsana*), with the head on the ground supported by the two arms with interlocked fingers. Once stable, slowly bend your legs into a diamond-shape so that the soles of the feet touch each other. In this pose, the body looks like a mace (*gadā*) or thunderbolt. Try to hold the pose for 1-2 minutes initially, gradually extending the time to

5-8 minutes. Slowly come out of the pose and then do the counterpose, *ārāsana* (fish pose), for a few minutes.

Benefits of Pose

- Improves overall circulation
- Impure blood from the legs and hips more efficiently reaches the heart and lungs for purification
- Increases circulation of fresh blood to the head, brain, eyes, ears, etc.
- Strengthens the throat and neck areas
- Spine becomes supple and strong

- Strengthens the generative organs
- May prevent the development of osteoporosis

Mantras

1. ॐ नमः धर्मनाथाय :: om namaḥ dharmanāthāya
2. णमो धम्माणं :: ṇamo dhammāṇaṁ
3. ॐ ह्रीम् श्रींम् नमः धर्मनाथाय प्रभवे मम ग्रह शान्ति कुरु कुरु स्वाहा :: om hrīm śrīm namaḥ dharmanāthāya prabhave mama graha śānti kuru kuru svāhā
4. ॐ ह्रीम् श्रींम् अर्हं श्रीं धर्मनाथाय नमः :: om hrīm śrīm arhaṁ śrī dharmanāthāya namaḥ

Benefits of *Mantras*

- Bring financial prosperity and abundance in agricultural commodities/food grains
- Make it possible to visit pilgrimage places
- Increase peacefulness in the family
- Alleviate affliction of and/or fortify Mercury
- Lord Dharmanātha protects the stomach and skeletal system of the body

INVOCATION

धर्म-तीर्थ-मनघं प्रवर्तयन् धर्म इत्यनु-मतः सतां भवान्

कर्म-कक्ष-मद-हत्तपोऽग्निभिः शर्म शाश्वत-मवाप शङ्करः

dharma-tīrtha-managhaṁ pravartayan dharma ityanu-mataḥ satāṁ bhavān

karma-kakṣa-mada-hattapo'gnibhiḥ śarma śāśvata-mavāpa śaṅkaraḥ

O Lord, you represent the unblemished abode of *dharma* and, as such, you have been conceived of as Dharmanātha which makes your name quite purposeful since you have burnt the forest of *karma*s with the fire of your *tapasya*, achieving everlasting bliss. You are also known by the name of Śaṅkara, which the wise people have also accepted.

- Svayaṁbhu Stotra (71)

Śāntiāsana

Lord Śāntinātha was born in Hastināpura. His father was King Viśvasena and his mother was Queen Achirā. At the time of Śāntinātha's birth, there was an extraordinary conjunction of planets in the *nakṣatra* of Bharaṇī. His place of *nirvāṇa* is Sammed Śikharji.

Prior to Śāntinātha's birth, plague was rampant in Hastināpura. But wherever the pregnant Achirā rested her gaze, the plague receded. Most of the city was spared from the plague. As a result, the child was called Śāntinātha, or the lord of peace. He became a great emperor (*cakravarti saṁrāṭa*) and eventually, the 16th Tīrthaṅkara.

In a previous life as King Megharatha, Śāntinātha had saved the life of a pigeon by offering a hungry hawk flesh from his own body. I have created a pose that looks like a flying pigeon in honour of Lord Śāntinātha, and have called it *śāntiāsana*.

Procedure

On a mat or on the ground, lie face down in a relaxed state. Bend both legs and place the straight arms over both ankles, with the right arm on the right ankle and left arm on the left ankle. Take a deep breath and lift the head, chest and knees off the ground while the arms are stretched and taut. Imagining your arms and legs to be wings, move your limbs up and down like a bird's wings. Try this pose for about 10 seconds. Breathe out and relax your body completely. Repeat 2-3 times.

Benefits of Pose

- Improves circulation in the whole body and makes the arms, legs and torso youthful and more flexible
- Makes the spinal vertebrae and ribs flexible and strong
- Reduces fat on the abdomen, arms and legs
- Reduces negative thoughts and improves self-confidence
- Reduces wastage of time and helps the *sādhaka* complete work more efficiently
- Improves quality of rest and sleep; reduces the need for sleep

Mantras

1. ॐ नमः शान्तिनाथाय :: om namaḥ śāntināthāya
2. णमो सान्तिणं :: ṇamo sāntiṇaṁ
3. ॐ ह्रीम् श्रीम् नमः शान्तिनाथाय प्रभवे मम ग्रह शान्ति कुरु कुरु स्वाहा :: om hrīm śrīm namaḥ śāntināthāya prabhave mama graha śānti kuru kuru svāhā
4. ॐ ह्रीम् श्रीम् अर्हं श्रीं शान्तिनाथाय नमः :: om hrīm śrīm arhaṁ śrī śāntināthāya namaḥ

Benefits of *Mantras*

- Help to control the diseases of cholera, malaria and vitiligo
- Calm the disturbances created by etheric beings
- Ensure a person's safe return from faraway places
- Increase bliss in the *sādhaka*
- Alleviate affliction of and/or fortify Mercury
- Lord Śāntinātha protects the navel and vital energy centres of the body

INVOCATION

विधाय रक्षां परतः प्रजानां राजा चिरं योऽप्रतिम-प्रतापः

व्यधात्पुरस्तात्स्वत एव शान्तिर् मुनिर्दयामूर्ति-रिवाऽघ-शान्तिम्

vidhāya rakṣyām parataḥ prajānāṃ rājā ciraṁ yo'pratima-pratāpaḥ

vyadhātyurastātsvata eva śāntir munirdayāmūrti-rivāgha-śāntim

Lord Śāntinātha had been a powerful *cakravarti* king earlier and protected his subjects from their enemies. He ruled for a long time. Subsequently, becoming averse to all worldly pleasures, he disowned his kingdom and became an ascetic full of compassion and mercy. Washing out all the evil *karma*s, he purified his soul.

- Svayaṁbhu Stotra (76)

Kunthuāsana

卐卐卐

Lord Kunthunātha was born in Hastināpura (Gajapura). His father was King Surasena and mother was Śrīdevī. Kunthunātha was the sixth great emperor of *Bhāratavarṣa* and his place of *nirvāṇa* is Sammed Śikharji.

Kunthunātha's symbol is the goat. Mountain goats are extremely agile. They arch their bodies like a bow, and may stand on three or even two legs on a steep cliff. The one-armed *cakrāsana* (wheel pose) invoked for me Lord Kunthunātha, so I have called that classic Haṭha Yoga pose *kunthuāsana*.

Procedure

Lie on the back and bend both legs so that the heels touch the buttocks. Bend the arms and place the palms on the ground overhead close to the shoulders, with the fingers facing the shoulders. Upon exhalation, lift the buttocks and back off the ground. The hands and feet will support the body. If you find this too challenging, you can place the top of the head on the ground for additional support. Slowly start reducing the distance between the fingers and the heels (eventually, they should touch) and the body will look like it is circular (*cakra*). Slowly lower your body to the ground and breathe in and out gently and slowly. Rest.

Tīrthaṅkarāsana

Variations (advanced):

1. Once you have mastered *cakrāsana*, carefully lift one hand off the ground and rest it on your thigh. Imagine yourself to be a goat with two feet and one hand on the ground. Chant *ṇamo kunthunaṁ* (see *mantra* section) while holding the pose. Bring the left arm down to the ground and repeat with the other hand.
2. While in *cakrāsana*, try lifting the left leg and place the left foot on the right knee. Bring it back down and try it with the other side.
3. Once you are comfortable with the variations above, then you can try to lift the left arm and right foot off the ground, and then vice versa. Please attempt this pose with supervision as it may be very difficult.

Benefits of Pose

- Reduces abdominal fat
- Makes the back supple and strong
- Reduces pain in the lower back and neck
- Balances *vāta doṣa*, thereby helping calf muscles (sometimes referred to as the second heart)
- Helps to soothe menstrual pains
- Helps to develop a strong and balanced mind in a strong and flexible body
- Strengthens arms, legs, ankles and wrists

Mantras

1. ॐ नमः कुन्थुनाथाय :: om namaḥ kunthunāthāya
2. णमो कुन्थुणं :: ṇamo kunthuṇaṁ
3. ॐ ह्रीम् श्रींम् नमः कुन्थुनाथाय प्रभवे मम ग्रह शान्ति कुरु कुरु स्वाहा :: om hrīm śrīm namaḥ kunthunāthāya prabhave mama graha śānti kuru kuru svāhā
4. ॐ ह्रीम् श्रींम् अर्हं श्रीं कुन्थुनाथाय नमः :: om hrīm śrīm arhaṁ śrī kunthunāthāya namaḥ

Benefits of *Mantras*

- Remove fear of enemies, bad-natured persons, criminals and cunning persons
- Calm various animals, including the bull, elephant, horse, and rabid animals
- Reduce the possibility of attack by wild animals such as bears, monkeys, lions, and tigers

- Alleviate affliction of and/or fortify Mercury
- Lord Kunthunātha protects the generative organs

INVOCATION

कुंथु-प्रभृत्य-खिल-सत्त्व-दयैक-तानः कुंथु र्जिनो ज्वर-जरा-मरणोप-शान्त्यै

त्वं धर्म-चक्र-मिह वर्तयसि स्म भूत्यै भूत्वा पुराक्षिति-पतीश्वर-चक्र-पाणि

kuṅthu-prabhṛtya-khila-sattva-dayaika-tānaḥ kuṅthur jino jvara-jarā-maraṇopa-śāntyai

tvaṁ dharma-cakra-miha vartayasi sma bhūtyai bhūtvā purākṣiti-patīśvara-cakra-pāṇi

O Lord, you had been the only one who extended his compassion equally to Kunthu and other creatures of the world. Your name is therefore fully justified as Kunthunātha. You attained the position of a *cakravarti* king and later turned into an ascetic and set the divine wheel of dharma rolling in order to propagate *mokṣa-lakṣmī*, which means freedom from disease, old-age and death.

- Svayaṁbhu Stotra (81)

Arāsana

卐卐

Lord Aranātha was born in Hastināpura. His father was King Sudarśana and his mother was Queen Mahādevī. Aranātha was born with a number of rare and auspicious symbols on his hands and feet, including *svastikas* on both palms and fish on both soles. He was the seventh universal emperor (*cakravarti saṁrāṭa*) of *bhāratavarṣa*. Because Aranātha established the four-fold *dharmasaṅgha*, he has been called the Bhāva Tīrthaṅkara as well as Bhāva Arihaṅta.

Aranātha protects the lower back and lower abdomen. The yogic fish pose (*matsyāsana*) protects the same, plus the hip socket. Due to the similarities, I have equated *matsyāsana* with *arāsana*.

Procedure

Sit in the lotus pose or *padmāsana*. Using the elbows, slowly lower the back to the floor. Place the palms under the buttocks. Pushing the elbows to the ground, lift the shoulders and back off the ground and turn the head backwards so that the top of the head is resting on the ground. Now push the shoulders further up and place the palms in *namaskāra* gesture on the heart area. Hold the pose for 10-15 seconds. Slowly increase the time to 3-5 minutes.

Tīrthaṅkarāsana

This is a counterpose for *śreyāṁśāsana* and *dharmāsana*, both of which are variations of the shoulder stand.

Benefits of Pose

- Improves blood circulation to head and brain
- Improves functioning of the pineal and pituitary glands in the head area as well as the thyroid and para-thyroid glands in the throat area
- Strengthens eyes, ears and sinuses
- Strengthens knee and hip joints, lower back, upper back and neck muscles
- Stimulates the colon and relieves constipation

Mantras

1. ॐ नमः अरनाथाय :: om namaḥ aranāthāya
2. णमो अराणं :: ṇamo arāṇaṁ

3. ॐ ह्रीम् श्रीम् नमः अरनाथाय प्रभवे मम ग्रह शान्ति कुरु कुरु स्वाहा :: om hrīm śrīm namaḥ aranāthāya prabhave mama graha śānti kuru kuru svāhā
4. ॐ ह्रीम् श्रीम् अर्हं श्रीं अरनाथाय नमः :: om hrīm śrīm arhaṁ śrī aranāthāya namaḥ

Benefits of *Mantra*s

- Help pacify displeased or angry ethereal beings, enemies, people in positions of power, and wild animals
- Alleviate affliction of and/or fortify Mercury
- *Sādhaka* gets victory in every endeavour
- Lord Aranātha strengthens and protects the lower back and abdomen

INVOCATION

मोह-रुपो रिपुः पापः, कषाय-भट-साधनः

दृष्टि-संपदु-पेक्षाऽस्त्रैस्त्वया धीर! पराजितः

moha-rupo ripuḥ papaḥ, kaṣāya-bhaṭa-sādhanaḥ

dṛṣṭi-saṁpadu-pekṣā'straistvayā dhīra! parājitaḥ

O the great patient and resolute Lord Ara Jinendra, by using the three dreaded weapons of right perception, right knowledge and right conduct, you have vanquished the formidable enemy of *mohaniya karma* which is armed with the deadly forces of lust, anger, passion, etc.

- Svayaṁbhu Stotra (90)

Malliāsana

卐卐卐卐

Mallinātha Devī[24] was born in Mithila. Her father's name was King Kumbharājā and her mother was Queen Prabhādevī. During pregnancy, Prabhādevī felt like sleeping on a bed of flowers. The majority of the flowers she chose were jasmine, otherwise known as *mālatī* flowers. Thus the infant was given the name Malli (*prakṛt* derivation of the Sanskrit *mālatī*). Her *lānchan* is the *kalaśa* (a pitcher or jar) with an *oṁ* symbol. Haṭha Yoga's *oṁkārāsana* is evocative of Mallinātha, so I have equated *oṁkārāsana* with *malliāsana*.

There is a temple dedicated to Mallinātha in Mannargudi, Tamil Nadu, which dates back to 250 BCE. Her *nirvāṇa* place is Sammed Śikharji.

---

[24] In the Śvetāmbara tradition, Mallinātha was female; in Digāmbara tradition, Mallinātha is male. To be able to write fluidly using pronouns, we will assume that Mallinātha was female without negating the opposite possibility. Lest one get too involved in the debate, remember that the ultimate beings of Jainism, *siddhas*, have no shape or body, and are thus genderless.

Procedure

This pose is extremely difficult – please be very careful when attempting it and ensure that someone else is with you.

Sit cross-legged. Place the toes of the left foot in the groin area. Slowly raise the right leg up. Initially, try to touch the forehead with the right foot. Then, try to touch the top of the head with the right foot. Finally, slide the right foot behind the neck. The back, neck and head should be in a straight line. Place your palms on the ground in front of you; you may also place them in front of you in a *namaskāra* gesture.

Repeat on the other side, that is, with left foot eventually on back of the neck.

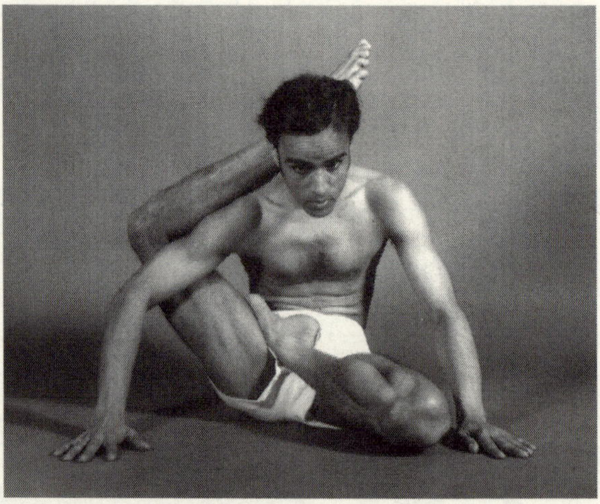

Very advanced Haṭha yogis can eventually put both feet behind the neck at the same time.

Benefits of Pose

- Develops a very high level of flexibility and strength in the ankles, knees and legs
- Improves circulation in the head, neck and back areas
- Stimulates all *cakras*; with closed eyes, practitioner may visualize inner lights and hear *anāhata nāda* (unstruck divine sounds)
- Helps the practitioner to enter into and remain in meditation or *dhyāna*, thereby hastening progress towards self realization

Mantras

1. ॐ नमः मल्लिनाथाय :: om namaḥ mallināthāya
2. णमो मल्लिणं :: ṇamo malliṇaṁ
3. ॐ ह्रीम् श्रींम् नमः मल्लिनाथाय प्रभवे मम ग्रह शान्ति कुरु कुरु स्वाहा :: om hrīm śrīm namaḥ mallināthāya prabhave mama graha śānti kuru kuru svāhā
4. ॐ ह्रीम् श्रींम् अर्हं भगवति मल्लिनाथाय नमः :: om hrīm śrīm arhaṁ bhagavati mallināthāya namaḥ

Benefits of *Mantras*

- Alleviate affliction of and/or fortify Ketu
- Balance water in the environment: offers protection from excessive rain and flooding and also brings rain when necessary
- Help the *sādhaka* to understand and thereby transcend ego

- Beneficial for all kinds of counsellors to help guide their clients in a proper direction
- Mallinātha Devī protects the chest (including the heart), back, spinal column, and legs

INVOCATION

यस्य महर्षेः सकल-पदार्थ-प्रत्यवबोधः समजनि साक्षात्

सामर-मर्त्यं जग-दपि सर्वं प्राञ्जलि भूत्वा प्रणिंपतति स्म

yasya maharṣeḥ sakala-padārtha-pratyavabodhaḥ samajani sākṣāt

samara-martyaṁ jaga-dapi sarvaṁ prāñjli bhūtvā praṇiṁpatati sma

Lord Mallinātha had been a great sage, who among all living and non-living beings achieved *kevalajñāna*. The entire world pays respectful homage to her with folded hands including gods and human beings alike. I humbly take refuge with the Lord.

- Svayaṁbhu Stotra (106)

MUNISUVRATĀSANA

卐卐

Lord Munisuvratanātha was born in Rājagṛha. His father was King Sumitra and his mother was Queen Prabhāvatī. While pregnant, Prabhāvatī observed many Jain vows resulting in the child being named *muni-su-vrata*, which can be translated as 'the excellent vows of the *munis*'. His *nirvāṇabhūmi* is Sammed Śikharji.

Legend asserts that Munisuvratanātha was a contemporary of Śrī Rāma.[25] His *lānchan* is the turtle, and he practiced many *yogāsanas* including *kurmāsana* (turtle pose) along with *dhyāna* enroute to *kevalajñāna*. Therefore, I have equated *kurmāsana* with *munisuvratāsana*.

Procedure

Sit in *vajrāsana*. Breathing out, bend forward and let the chest go down towards the thighs. The heels of the feet should be touching and the feet spread outwards in a V-shape. Place the palms next to the knees. Breathing in, lift the head high, look straight ahead and elongate the neck like a turtle. Contract the

---

[25] According to Vālmiki's Rāmāyana, King Daśaratha received Jaina *śramanas* as royal guests. Rāma, Lakṣamana, and Rāvaṇa are mentioned amongst the 63 eminent personages in Ācārya Hemacandra's *Triṣaṣthisalaka Purūṣa*. There is evidence of mutual admiration and interchange between ancient Jainism and Hinduism.

muscles of the entire body, then relax and breathe out slowly pushing the forehead towards the floor. Repeat this action 9-11 times.

Benefits of Pose

- Helps reduce abdominal fat and tone the stomach
- Strengthens the legs including the thighs (hamstring muscles), hip and knee joints
- Reduces lower back pain and calms irritated sciatica nerves

- By strengthening and toning the neck muscles and nerves, may alleviate headaches
- May reduce facial and neck wrinkles
- Alleviates eyestrain caused by excessive screen time, reading, poor lighting, etc.
- Relieves problems with the stomach and gallbladder
- Improves digestion and elimination of toxic waste products

Mantras

1. ॐ नमः मुनिसुव्रतनाथाय :: om namaḥ munisuvratanāthāya
2. णमो मुनिसुव्वयाणं :: ṇamo munisuvvayāṇaṁ
3. ॐ ह्रीम् श्रींम् नमः मुनिसुव्रत प्रभवे मम ग्रह शान्ति कुरु कुरु स्वाहा :: om hrīm śrīm namaḥ munisuvrata prabhave mama graha śānti kuru kuru svāhā
4. ॐ ह्रीम् श्रींम् अर्हं श्रीं मुनिसुव्रताय नमः :: om hrīm śrīm arhaṁ śrī munisuvratāya namaḥ

Benefits of *Mantras*

- Alleviate affliction of and/or fortify Saturn
- Reduce or remove problems created by ethereal beings
- Relieve troubles originating from the government
- Lord Munisuvratanātha protects the thighs

INVOCATION

तणुगंधें जो सनु चंदणासु चंदणासु पउणइ जो तेयं चंदणासु

जो पणमिउ रामें लक्खणेण धम्मेण अहिंसालक्खणेण

taṇugaṅdheṁ jo sanu caṅdaṇāsu caṅdanāsu pauṇai jo teyaṁ caṅdaṇāsu

jo paṇamiu rameṁ lakkhaṇeṇa dhammeṇa ahiṁsālakkhaṇeṇa

[I bow to Lord Munisuvrata] whose body has the fragrance of sandalwood, who can humble the moon with his lustre, who has been adored by Rāma and Lakṣamaṇa, who has helped people to achieve *mokṣa* by following the path of *ahiṁsā*.

- Mahāpurāṇa 68.1

NAMIĀSANA

卐卐

Lord Naminātha was born in Mithila, the son of King Vijayasena and Queen Vipradevī. His feet were marked with the symbol of the blue lotus. During the Vipradevī's pregnancy, Mithila was attacked by its enemies resulting in great danger to the kingdom. The Queen gazed upon the attacking army from the heights of the palace, and incredibly, the entire army laid down their arms, bowed to and saluted the Queen. Because of this miraculous event, Vijayasena named his son Naminātha (*nami* means to bow or bend down).

In the ninth chapter of the *Uttaradhyāyana Sutra*, Lord Mahāvīra refers to Naminātha as Lord even while he was a householder.[26] Even though a householder, Naminātha bloomed like a lotus due to his right knowledge, right perception, right conduct, and right *tapa*. Therefore, for us, Haṭha Yoga's blooming lotus pose (*vikasita kamalāsana*) becomes *namiāsana*.

Lord Naminātha's *nirvāṇabhūmi* is Sammed Śikharji.

---

[26] Hinduism accords a similarly honoured place to householder yogis (Śrī Lahiri Mahāśāya is but one of many examples). A householder yogi maintains unwavering focus on Truth and Self even while fulfilling worldly duties.

Procedure

Sit on a mat with legs bent. Place the right palm under the right heel and the left palm under the left heel. Straighten both legs. In the beginning, it may be difficult to straighten the legs; practice diligently to make them straight. The entire body should be balanced on the buttocks. The legs and arms on either side should resemble two open petals of a lotus flower, with the head resembling an unopened bud.

When first practicing, it may be hard to hold the pose perfectly still. You may roll on the back or on either side. Do not give up trying to become perfectly still. Try to practice the pose with complete stillness for 5-6 minutes, chanting a Naminātha *mantra*.

Benefits of Pose

- Allows one to focus and concentrate the mind
- The mind becomes balanced and does not wander from thought to thought
- Increases flexibility of arms, legs and hips
- Improves the functioning of the stomach, pancreas and colon
- Reduces fat from the legs, abdomen and buttocks
- Reduces pain in the knees and shoulders
- May alleviate urinary tract infections

Mantras

1. ॐ नमः नमिनाथाय :: om namaḥ namināthāya
2. णमो नमिणं :: ṇamo namiṇaṁ
3. ॐ ह्रीम् श्रींम् नमः नमिनाथाय प्रभवे मम ग्रह शान्ति कुरु कुरु स्वाहा :: om hrīm śrīm namaḥ namināthāya prabhave mama graha śānti kuru kuru svāhā
4. ॐ ह्रीम् श्रींम् अर्हं श्रीं नमिनाथाय नमः :: om hrīm śrīm arhaṁ śrī namināthāya namaḥ

Benefits of *Mantras*

- Improve relations with elite government and corporate officials
- Alleviate affliction of and/or fortify Mercury
- Lord Naminātha protects the toes, feet and legs

INVOCATION

स्तुतिः स्तोतुः साधोः कुशल-परिणा-माय स तदा,

भवेन् मा वा स्तुत्यः फलमपि ततस्तस्य च सतः

किमेवं स्वाधीन्याज् जगति सुलभे श्रायस-पथे,

स्तुयान् न त्वा विद्वान् सतत-मपि पूज्यंनमि जिनम्

stutiḥ stotuḥ sādhoḥ kuśala-pariṇā-māya sa tadā,

bhaven mā vā stutyaḥ phalamapi tatastasya ca sataḥ

kimevaṁ svādhīnyāj jagati sulabhe śrāyasa-pathe,

stuyāna na tvā vidvān satata-mapi pūjyaṁnami jinam

The deity who is being worshipped may or may not be present at the time and the place of worship. Similarly, the one who worships may not be bestowed with the desired gift from the deity who is being worshipped. But one thing is sure that the one who worships surely is bestowed with the virtue and the moral strength to purify his soul. Thus the path of bliss is directly available to the worshipper. Then who would be unwise enough not to adore Lord Naminātha?

- Svayambhu Stotra (116)

NEMIĀSANA

卐卐卐卐

Lord Neminātha is alternatively and commonly known by his full name of Ariṣṭanemi. He was born in Śauripūra (Dvārakā). His father was King Samudravijaya, his grandfather was King Andhakavṛṣni, and his mother was Queen Śivādevī. Samudravijaya was the brother of Vasudeva, the father of Lord Kṛṣṇa, thus making Neminātha and Śrī Kṛṣṇa first cousins. Neminātha may have lived around 3,500 BCE and there is evidence that he was a historical figure.[27]

---

[27] In addition to the linkages with Śrī Kṛṣṇa, Professor Alois Anton Führer has put forth evidence of Neminātha's historicity based on excavations at Kankali Tila (mound) near Mathura. There are references to Neminātha in the Mahābhārata (vanaparva 184,8 and śantiparva 288/5,46) and in the Ṛgveda. There are references to Ariṣṭanemi in the Yajurveda (where he is referred to as an important *ṛṣi*, capable of crossing over the ocean of life and death) and in the Sāmaveda as well. The Harivaṁśa Purāṇa contains references to Ariṣṭanemi. A linkage between the great Babylonian king Nebuchadnezzar and Neminātha has also been suggested. The Chhandogya Upaniṣada (III, 7, 6) speaks of a Ghora Āṅgirasa who taught Lord Kṛṣṇa and as his guru-dakṣina, asked him to live in simplicity, be non-violent, and be truthful. (It is interesting to note that Lord Kṛṣṇa did not physically take up arms in the Mahābhārata war, choosing to remain a charioteer and advisor.) Because these teachings are similar to the tenets of Jainism, there are

Kṛṣṇa was instrumental in arranging the marriage of Neminātha to Rājīmatī (Rājulakumari). However, after witnessing the violence involved in preparing so many animals for slaughter for the wedding feast, Neminātha renounced the idea of marriage and all worldly life, and took *dikṣa*. Rājīmatī also took *dikṣa*. The Jaina *āgamas* portray this story in an elaborate and beautiful fashion.

Neminātha's *nirvāṇa* happened on the 8th day of the bright half of *Āṣāḍha* at Mount Girnar (also known as Revatagiri) in Gujarat. Lord Neminātha's *lānchan* is the conch shell.

In honour of the linkages between Śrī Kṛṣṇa and Neminātha, I equate the Haṭha Yoga pose of *kṛṣṇāsana* with *nemiāsana*.

---

suggestions that Neminātha may have been identical with the Hindu sage Ghora Āṅgirasa, and/or that Śrī Kṛṣṇa was a pupil of both Neminātha and Ghora Āṅgirasa. Neminātha also foresaw the destruction of Dvārakā, which even Kṛṣṇa could not prevent.

Procedure

This pose is extremely difficult and should be undertaken with caution and under expert guidance. Stand straight on level ground. Stretching carefully, place the left foot on the neck. Bend forward. Slowly extend the right leg as far as you can. Lift the right hand off the ground and extend it overhead. Hold this pose for a maximum of 10-15 seconds. Repeat with the right foot on the neck, keeping the left leg and right arm on the ground. Women should avoid this pose during the menstrual period.

Benefits of Pose

- The *sādhaka* may receive seemingly miraculous benefits depending on the prevailing *guṇa* in the *sādhaka: sattva, rājas, tamas*
    - For example, this pose will facilitate the opening of the esoteric *cakras*, thus opening the doors for spiritual progression, increase in intuitive abilities, and the development of special gifts and powers (*siddhis*, especially *vāk siddhi*)
- The entire body becomes flooded with vitality
- The muscles of the arms and legs develop beautifully, becoming bulked up and flexible
- Improves confidence and will-power
- Improves the condition of the blood vessels, muscles and nerves of the feet, knees, hip joints, legs, arms, neck and shoulders

Art of Blowing the Conch Shell

As the conch shell is the symbol of Lord Neminātha, this is an appropriate place to describe this ancient and powerful practice. Every Hindu temple priest, for example, blows a conch shell before *ārati*.

Find a good-sized conch shell with a hole allowing one to blow air through it. Every morning, blow the shell for at least 20-25 seconds, or as long as possible. Slowly increase the time of exhalation. Keep experimenting until you can produce a sustained sound (it may not be easy at first).

Benefits: increases the power of the lungs; helps alleviate asthma, allergies & bronchitis; improves the tone and power of the facial muscles, thus enabling better playing of wind instruments, etc.

Mantras

1. ॐ नमः नेमिनाथाय :: om namaḥ neminathāya
2. णमो नेमिणं :: ṇamo nemiṇaṁ
3. ॐ ह्रीम् श्रीम् नमः अरिष्टनेमिय प्रभवे मम ग्रह शान्ति कुरु कुरु स्वाहा :: om hrım śrīm namaḥ ariṣṭanemiya prabhave mama graha śānti kuru kuru svāhā
4. ॐ ह्रीम् श्रीम् अर्हं श्रीं अरिष्टनेमिय नमः :: om hrīm śrīm arhaṁ śrī ariṣṭanemiya namaḥ

Benefits of *Mantras*

- Alleviate affliction of and/or fortify Rāhu
- Reduce or remove the effects of negative *karma*, especially when one is going through difficulties, sickness, and/or general problems in life
- Allow the *sādhaka* to fulfil hopes and aspirations
- Lord Ariṣṭanemi protects both feet and legs

INVOCATION

भगवा-नृषिः परम-योग-दहन-हुत-कल्मषेन्धनः

ज्ञान-विपुल-किरणैः सकलं प्रतिबुद्धय बुद्ध-कमलायतेक्षणः

हरिवंश-केतु-रन-नद्य-विनय-दम-तीर्थ-नायकः

शील-जलधि-रभवो विभवस्त्व-मरिष्ट-नेमि-जिन-कुन्जरोऽजरः

bhagavā-nṛṣiḥ parama-yoga-dahana-huta-kalmaṣendhanaḥ

jñāna-vipula-kiraṇaiḥ sakalaṁ pratibuddhaya buddha-kamalāyatekṣaṇaḥ

harivaṁśa-ketu-rana-nadya-vinaya-dama-tīrtha-nāyakaḥ

śīla-jaladhi-rabhavo vibhavastva-mariṣṭa-nemi-jina-kuṁjaro'jaraḥ

Lord Neminātha is adored by Indra and other gods. He is endowed with the supreme *ṛddhis* [supernatural powers] and has burnt all the *karmic* wood in the fire of *śukla-dhyāna*. His eyes are like the blossomed lotus flowers. He is the head of the Hari dynasty and the source of scriptures which advocate humility and control of the senses. He is the ocean of virtues and free from old age. You illuminated the entire world by the rays of *kevalajñāna* and attained *mokṣa*.

- Svayaṁbhu Stotra (121-122)

Pārśvāsana

卐

Lord Pārśvanātha was born around 872 BCE in Vārāṇasi on the 10th day of the dark-half of the month of *Pauṣa*.[28] His father was King Aśvasena and his mother was Queen Vāmādevī. He achieved *nirvāṇa* at the age of 100 at what is now known as Pārśvanātha Hill, Sammed Śikharji.

In the era of Pārśvanātha, many ascetics engaged in practices of *tapasya* that, often inadvertently, were cruel and harmful to other living beings. Once, Pārśvanātha rescued a pair of snakes from the *dhūni* of a *sādhu* named Kamaṭh. The snakes, who heard the *mantra* A-SI-Ā-U-SĀ from Pārśvanātha, became Dhāranendra and Padmāvatī (the accompanying deities of Lord Pārśvanātha) and subsequently protected Pārśvanātha from Meghalin (the reborn Kamaṭh) and troubles created by ethereal beings. Combined with the fact that Pārśvanātha's *lānchan* is the cobra, Haṭha yoga's *bhujangāsana* or cobra pose can be called *pārśvāsana*.

[28] According to modern convention and *pace* the commentary for Neminātha, Pārśvanātha is the only Tīrthaṅkara apart from Mahāvīra Svāmi who can definitively be called a historical figure. Zarathustra of Persia was said to have been a contemporary of Pārśvanātha.

Procedure

Lie on a mat or the ground face down with the feet together. Place both palms near the shoulders with the fingers facing forwards. Breathing in, slowly lift the head and spine up and straighten the arms. Only the hips, legs & palms should be touching the ground. Hold for 10-15 seconds. Breathe out and slowly come down. Repeat several times, each time bringing the hands about an inch back. In the beginning, you may use the arms to push yourself up; later, the spine alone should become strong enough to support your weight.

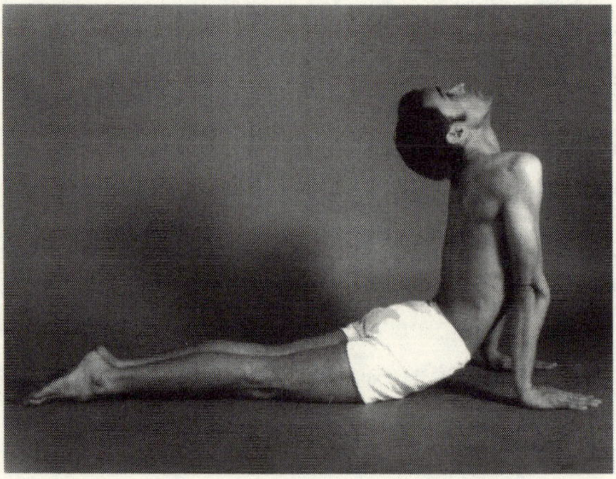

Benefits of Pose

- The whole spine gets stretched, toned and more flexible
- The spinal nerves become less restricted, thus improving the function of the digestive organs
- Helps the hips and back as well as the internal organs of the lower and upper abdomen

- Alleviates menstrual difficulties
- Strengthens the hands, wrists, shoulders, rib cage, diaphragm and neck
- Tones and strengthens the heart and lungs
- Helps strengthen and tone the chest muscles

Mantras

1. ॐ नमः पार्श्वनाथाय :: om namaḥ pārśvanāthāya
2. णमो पासणं :: ṇamo pāsaṇaṁ
3. ॐ ह्रीम् श्रींम् नमः पार्श्वनाथाय प्रभवे मम ग्रह शान्ति कुरु कुरु स्वाहा :: om hrīm śrīm namaḥ pārśvanāthāya prabhave mama graha śānti kuru kuru svāhā
4. ॐ ह्रीम् श्रींम् अर्हं श्रीं पार्श्वनाथाय नमः :: om hrīm śrīm arhaṁ śrī pārśvanāthāya namaḥ

Benefits of *Mantras*

- Relieve affliction of and/or fortify Ketu in the *sādhaka's* horoscope
- Resolve problems with the state, ethereal beings, and wild animals
- Fulfil positive desires of the mind
- Lord Pārśvanātha protects the entire body

INVOCATION

स सत्य-विद्या-तपसां प्रणायकः समग्रधी-रुग्र-कुलाम्बरांशुमान्

मया सदा पार्श्व-जिनः प्रणम्यते विलीन-मिथ्या-पथ-दृष्टि-विभ्रमः

sa satya-vidyā-tapasāṁ praṇāyakaḥ samagradhī-rugra-kulāmbarāṁśumān

mayā sadā pārśva-jinaḥ praṇamyate vilīna-mithyā-patha-dṛṣṭi-vibhramaḥ

O Lord, you propounded true sciences and meditation. You achieved *kevalajñāna*, are omniscient and are the great son of the Ugra dynasty. You are the remover of delusion emanating from disbelief. O Lord Pārśvanātha, I offer my salutation to you again and again.

- Svayambhu Stotra (135)

MAHĀVĪRĀSANA

卐

Lord Mahāvīrasvāmi, the 24th and final Tīrthaṅkara of the present era, was born on the 13th day of the bright half of the month of *Caitra* in *hasta nakṣatra* in Kṣatriyakuṇḍa, a suburb of the city of Vaiśāli in modern-day Bihar. His skin tone was golden and his *lānchan* was that of the lion. Lord Mahāvīra's father's name was King Siddhārtha and his mother was Queen Triśalādevī. During the Queen's pregnancy, there was a generalized increase in prosperity and abundance in the kingdom so the baby was named Vardhamāna, which means 'growing/thriving/ prospering'. He was subsequently given the name Mahāvīra, meaning 'Great Hero'.

During the time of Mahāvīra, sacrificial *yajñas* were common and caused violence and harm to animals and the environment. The status of women was low. The natural order of human society was degrading.

Mahāvīra lived as a householder for the first 30 years of his life. After the death of his parents and with the permission of his elder brother, he took *vṛata* (vows) and wandered for 12.5 years, undergoing many severe penances. He would fast for six months at a stretch. He engaged in *sarvatobhadra pratimā*, *mahābhadra pratimā* and other very difficult yogic practices for many years. Mahāvīra became a *kevalin* while in the yogic pose of *goduhāsana*, or the cow-milking pose. Lord Mahāvīra then preached the fundamental tenets of Jainism for the next 32 years. He restored some of the lost status of women by creating the female monastic category of *sādhvi* as well as the female householder category of *śrāvikā*. People from all walks of life – outcastes, low caste, high caste, kings, queens, Āryan, non-Āryan, *brahmaṇas*, etc. – all joined his *dharma saṅgha*.

Lord Mahāvīra was the last Tīrthaṅkara of this era. His *nirvāṇa* was on the new moon day of the month of *Kārtika* at Pāvāpuri. Jainas celebrate this day as Dīpāvalī.

In honour of Lord Mahāvīra's proximity to our time and place, I have selected two poses to represent him: *mahāvīrāsana* (Hanumāna's pose; Mahāvīra is also an epithet of Lord Rāma's faithful servant) and *siṁhāsana* or the lion pose (after Lord Mahāvīra's symbol).

Procedure

For mahāvīrāsana: Stand on a mat. Place the right foot forward, approximately three feet ahead of the left, with the knee bent slightly. Keep the left leg straight. Make fists with both hands, bend the arms, and while breathing in, pull the bent arms backwards and push the chest forwards. Hold the pose for 15-20 seconds. While breathing out, let the whole body relax. Repeat this on the opposite side. As you do this pose, visualize that the energy and power of Mahāvīra–Hanumāna is surging through every muscle of your body.

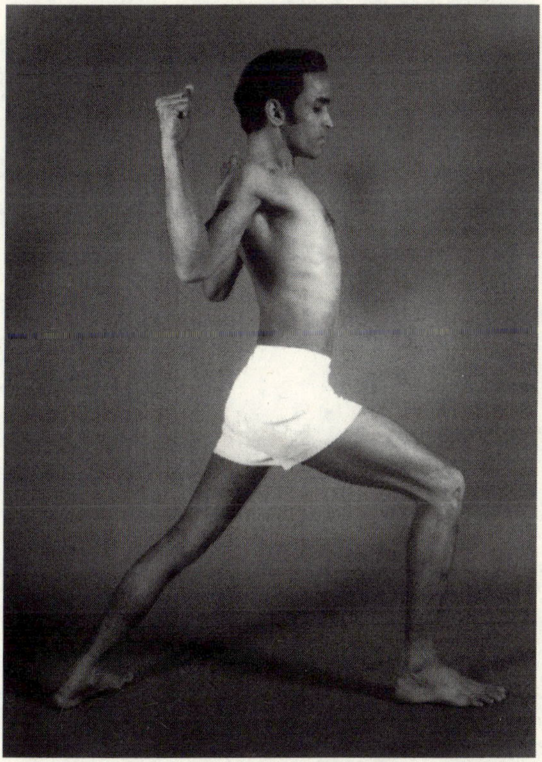

For siṁhāsana: Sit in *vajrāsana* (toes together and heels apart with approximately 8-10 inches gap between the two knees; buttocks should rest on the heels of the feet). Spread the fingers of the palms and rest them on the thighs. Open your mouth wide and stick the tongue out like a lion/cat. Keep your eyes wide open. Stiffen your hands (with fingers spread out) and body and make an angry face as if you are about to attack. Stick the tongue out all the way and exhale forcefully. Maintain this pose for about

10-15 seconds until the point of coughing. Pull the tongue in, close the mouth and relax. Repeat this action three times.

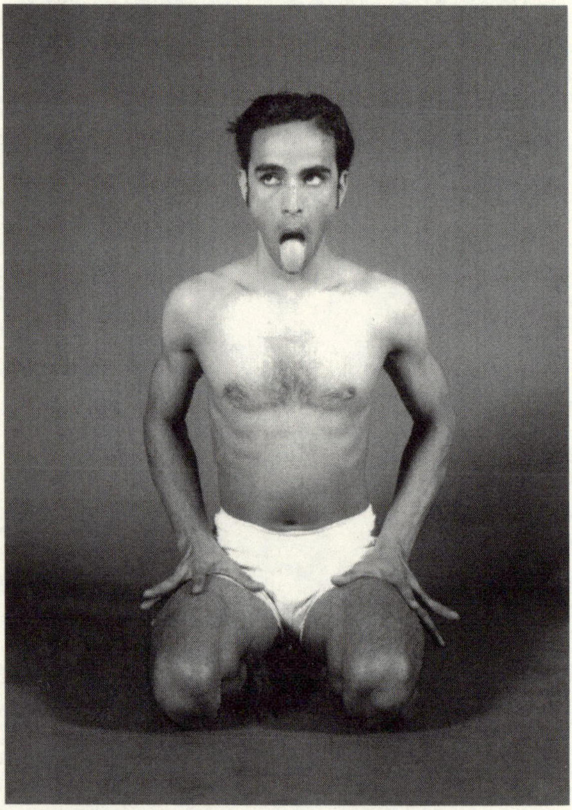

Benefits of Poses

Mahāvīrāsana:

- Improves circulation in the entire body
- Makes the chest wide and strong
- Reduces pain in the hip joint, back, neck & knees

- The opening of the chest allows the breath to penetrate deeper into the body, thus providing vital energy to every cell
- Good for rejuvenating weak organs

Siṁhāsana:

- Reduces lines around the lips, cheeks & eyes
- Makes the face and eyes youthful
- Head, face & throat get renewed energy
- Alleviates symptoms of cold, cough & flu
- Exercises the tongue, thereby improving the quality of the voice, speech and singing ability
- Increases secretion of saliva, thus aiding digestion
- Improves the functioning of the thyroid, parathyroid and adenoid glands

Mantras

1. ॐ नमः वर्धमानाय :: om namaḥ vardhamānāya
2. णमो वद्धमाणं :: ṇamo vaddhamāṇaṁ
3. ॐ ह्रीं श्रीं णमो वर्धमानाय प्रभवे मम ग्रह शान्ति कुरु कुरु स्वाहा :: om hrīṁ śrīṁ ṇamo vardhamānāya prabhave mama graha śānti kuru kuru svāhā
4. ॐ ह्रीं श्रीं अर्हं श्री वर्धमानाय नमः :: om hrīṁ śrīṁ arhaṁ śrī vardhamānāya namaḥ

Benefits of *Mantras*

- Alleviate affliction of and/or fortify Mercury

- Increase wealth, grain stocks, horses, elephants
- Promote happiness and health
- Lord Mahāvīrasvāmi protects the *ātma* (soul) through the light of knowledge

INVOCATION

त्व-मसि सुरासुर-महितो ग्रन्थिक-सत्त्वाशय-प्रणामाऽमहितः

लोक-त्रय-परम-हितो ऽनावरण-ज्योति-रुज्जवलद्-धाम-हितः

tva-masi surāsura-mahito granthika-sattvāśaya-
praṇāmā'mahitaḥ

loka-traya-parama-hito 'nāvaraṇa-jyoti-rujjavalad-dhāma-hitaḥ

O Śrī Vīra Jinendra, you are worshipped by gods and demons alike, but you are not revered by the impure and the misguided. You are the greatest well-wisher of all beings in the three worlds and have attained *mokṣa*, illumined by the light of *kevalajñāna*.

- Svayaṁbhu Stotra (139)

ARIHAṄTĀSANA

卐卐

The first line of the *Ṇamokāra Mahā Mantra* salutes the *arihaṅta* (*arhaṅta*), those exalted beings that have conquered all of their inner enemies and negativities. When, on the path to *mokṣa*, a being destroys the *ghaṭi karma*s that obscure correct knowledge; that obscure correct perception; that obscure correct reason & discrimination; and that prevent the doing and receiving of good deeds; that being is given the superlative and glorious title of *arihaṅta*.

Haṭha yoga has a pose called *prāṇāsana*. Only a person who has gained control over the ten *prāṇas* of the body can subdue negative qualities such as attachment, anger, ego, jealousy, and delusion. As *prāṇāsana* evokes the qualities of an *arihaṅta*, I have equated it with *arihaṅtāsana*.

Procedure

Sit on a yoga mat or the floor (but not a hard surface). Place the sole of the left foot in the right groin area. Bend the right leg and bring the heel to the buttock. Place the right hand on the right foot. Grab the right big toe with the right hand. Place the left hand on the left knee and sit as straight as you can. Breathe in, hold the breath (*kuṁbhaka*), and make the body stiff. After 15-20 seconds, breathe out and relax the whole body. Slowly increase the time of breath retention. Reverse the leg position to do the opposite form of this pose.

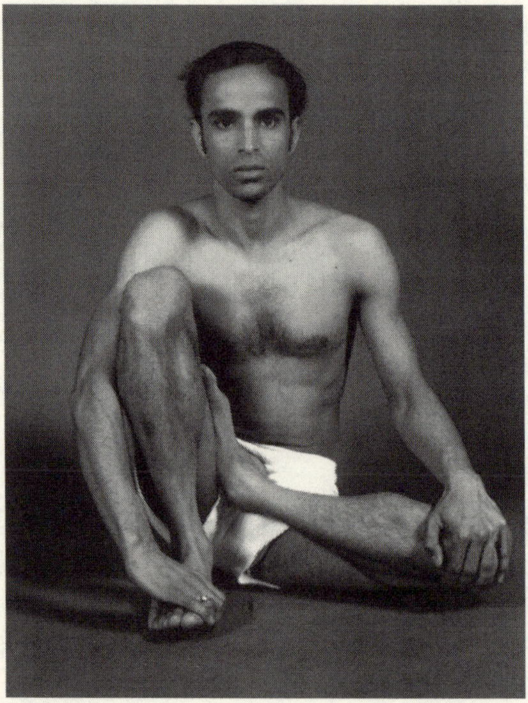

Benefits of Pose

- Feet and legs become flexible and strong
- Reduces abdominal fat
- Helps normalize and balance the pulse and blood pressure
- The big toe is linked to the pineal and pituitary glands as well as to the brain; esoterically, it is also the seat of pure divine nectar (*aṅguṣṭe amṛuta base*). Holding and thus

stimulating the big toe may help alleviate glandular problems and may relieve headaches

- Facilitates the flow of all ten *prāṇas* (vital airs of the body; five internal and five external), gently directing their energies to the higher energetic centres (*cakras*)

Mantras

*if possible, use a white *mālā* when reciting any of these *mantras**

1. णमो अरिहंताणं :: ṇamo arihaṅtāṇaṁ
2. ॐ ह्रीं णमो अरिहंताणं :: om hrīṁ ṇamo arihaṅtāṇaṁ
3. ॐ ह्रीं श्रीं अर्हं अर्हद्भ्यो णमो नमः :: om hrīṁ śrīṁ arhaṁ arhadbhyo ṇamo namaḥ
4. ॐ ह्रीं अर्हं नमः क्षीं स्वाहा :: om hrīṁ arhaṁ namaḥ kṣīṁ svāhā

Benefits of *Mantras*

- Alleviate affliction of and/or fortify the Moon and Venus
- *Arihaṅta Bhagavāna* protects the head and the brain
- Chanting अर्हं - 'arhaṁ' 400 times (or four *mālās*) gives the benefits of one *upavāsa* (fast)

Note Here are three variants of the first line of the *Ṇamokāra Mahā Mantra*:

1. ṇamo arihaṅtāṇaṁ - I salute that soul which is the conqueror of all inner enemies

2. ṇamo aruhaṅtāṇaṁ - I salute that soul which will not be born again
3. ṇamo arahantāṇaṁ - I salute that soul which is worthy of worship

The third form has been found in the Udayagirī/Khaṅḍagirī caves in modern-day Orissa dating back to 200 BCE.

In fact, according to the *Śrī-mantra-rajā-guṇa-kalpa-mahodadhi* of Śrī Jinakīrti Suri Mahārāja, a rare book published around 1920, there are 110 variants of the first line of the Ṇamokāra Mantra.

INVOCATION

नमो श्री अरिहन्त, करमां को कियो अन्त, हुआ सो केवलवंत करुणा भंडारी हैं

अतिशय चौंतीस धार, पैतीस वाणी उच्चार समझावे नर-नार, पर उपकारी हैं

namo śrī arihanta, karmāṅ ko kiyo anta, huā so kevalavaṅta karuṇā bhaṅḍārī hai

atiśaya cauṅtīsa dhāra, paitīsa vāṇī uccāra samajhāve nara-nāra, par upakārī hai

I give my obeisance to the *arihaṅtas*, who have ended the four *ghaṭi* karmas, acquired *kevalajñāna*, and who are the storehouses of compassion. They have 34 extraordinary qualities; their speech has 35 excellent qualities. They explain the *āgāmic* knowledge to males and females and they are always helping others on the spiritual path.

- Pratikramaṇasutra

Siddhāsana

卐卐

The second line of the *Ṇamokāra Mantra* pays obeisance to the *siddhas*. The term *siddha* is widely used in the Indian religious context to refer to a being of exalted spiritual accomplishment. Jainism takes the concept of *siddha* a step further. *Siddhas* are those beings that have attained the ultimate state of existence and are beyond all mundane qualities. They exist without body (and are thus genderless) as pure Soul, in continuous practice of *śukla-dhyāna* (the highest and purest form of meditation). Having exhausted the eight forms of *karma*, a *siddha* has gone beyond birth and death.

Once a being exhausts four types of *karma*, it becomes an *arihaṅta*. Once the remaining four types of *karma* are exhausted, the being becomes a *siddha*, enjoying everlasting bliss and peace. For a *siddha*, there is no attachment or aversion, so they are termed as *vītarāga*. Having conquered all negative emotions, they are *nirvikāra*. Knowing past, present and future, they are *sarvajña*.

Haṭha Yoga has a pose called *siddhāsana*, a seated pose which directly stimulates the flow of *prāṇa* energy from the root *cakra* and is particularly conducive to meditation and opening of the *cakras*. It is therefore apt to equate this pose with the Jaina *siddhāsana*.

Procedure

Sit on a clean mat. Bring the right heel into the perineum (the area between scrotum and anus for males; between vagina and anus for females) and place it there firmly. The heel of the foot should be pressing on the perineum and the sole of the right foot touching the inside of the left thigh. Bring the left foot in and place it on top of the right foot so that it is also touching the inside of the thigh. Hold the heel at that spot firmly. Both knees should touch the floor. Roll your eyes towards the centre of the eyebrows. Bend both index fingers and touch the fingertips to the tips of the thumbs (*jñānamudra*).

Hold the body and mind as steady as possible in this pose. It may take a long time before you can comfortably hold this pose. People who have difficulty observing sexual continence (*brahmacārya*) should only do this pose for a short time (less than one minute). Those with greater control can increase the time from one to three minutes. *Siddhāsana* is excellent for *sādhakas*, monks, nuns, and anyone on the path of self-realization.

Benefits of Pose

- This pose helps a person facilitate the correct performance of *mūlabaṅdha*
- Opens up the *suṣumna* or central esoteric nervous channel by facilitating the opening of the six *cakras*
- Regular and proper practice will calm and dissipate excessive bodily passion
- For males, reduces the incidence of nocturnal emissions, thus aiding in adherence to celibacy
- Pushes the semen and equivalent/related vital forces upwards
- The mind becomes one-pointed; *dhāraṇa* and *dhyāna* become deep and blissful[29]

Mantras

1. ॐ णमो सिद्धाणं (२) सिद्धाणं सिद्धाणं सिद्धाणं सिद्धाणं (२) :: om ṇamo siddhāṇaṁ (2) siddhāṇaṁ siddhāṇaṁ siddhāṇaṁ siddhāṇaṁ (2)
2. ॐ ह्रीं णमो सिद्धाणं :: om hrīṁ ṇamo siddhāṇaṁ

---

[29] With the eyes closed, the third eye may permit you to see a kaleidoscope of inner lights, especially when turning the eyes towards the centre of the eyebrows. (Turning the eyes to the tip of the nose, as suggested in other methodologies, may delay the seeing of the internal lights).

3. ॐ ह्रीं श्रीं अर्हं सिद्धेभ्यो णमो नमः :: om hrīṁ śrīṁ arhaṁ siddhebhyo ṇamo namaḥ
4. ॐ नमः सिद्धेभ्यो :: om namaḥ siddhebhyo

Benefits of *Mantra*s

- *Siddhas* protect the eyes, mouth-teeth, forehead (and third eye)
- *Mantra* #2 alleviates affliction of and/or fortifies Sun and Mars
- *Mantra* #4: to relieve fever – take a red shawl/blanket in the hands, chant this *mantra* eight times, and cover yourself.

INVOCATION

सकल करम टाल, वश कर लियो काल, मुगति में रहया माल,

आतमा को तारी है

अचल, अटल रूप, आवो नहीं भवकूप, अनुप सरुप ऊप, ऐसे सिद्ध धारी है

sakala karama ṭāla, vaśa kar liyo kāla, mugati me rahayā māla, ātamā ko tārī hai

acala, aṭala rūpa, āvo nahīṅ bhavakūpa, anupa sarūpa ūpa, aise siddha dhārī hai

Siddhas have annihilated all eight karmas and have conquered birth, sickness, old age, death, sorrow and poverty. They live on top of the universe in *siddhasīla* in the purest state of Soul. They are immobile, stable in form, and do not fall into the mundane wells of *saṁsāra*. They are bodiless and invisible. They have eight qualities – infinite knowledge, infinite perception, infinite bliss, infinite good character, undiminishing existence, formlessness, no heaviness or lightness, and infinite power.

- Pratikramaṇasutra

Āyariyāsana

卐卐

The third line of the *Ṇamokāra Mantra* honours the *ācāryas*[30] or heads of congregations. *Ācāryas* are a vital link between the teachings of the Jinas and the Jain laity, and are responsible for the preservation and propagation of Jaina *dharma*, including the *pañca mahāvratas*: non-violence; truthfulness; not to take anything that is not yours (including one's own identity); control of the senses and non-possession. *Ācāryas* guide and encourage the *sādhus* (monks), *sādhvis* (nuns), *śrāvakas* (male householders) and *śrāvikās* (female householders). We know of a number of illustrious *ācāryas* of the Jaina tradition, dating back to the time of Lord Mahāvīra and extending into the present era.

Matsyendranātha was one of the greatest *ācāryas* of the Haṭha yoga/Nāthapaṅtha lineage. To honour this superlative individual and his stature as a leader of Haṭha yogis, as well as to honour *ācāryas* everywhere and throughout time, I term the pose honouring him (*matsyendrāsana*) as *āyariyāsana*.

---

[30] *Āyaria* in the Jain scriptural language of *ardhamāgadhī*

Procedure

Sit on a clean mat. Bend the right leg and place the heel to the perineum. Bend the left leg bringing the left foot over the bent right knee, and place the left foot firmly on the ground. Now bring the straight right arm in between the left knee and chest and hold the left ankle firmly with the right hand. Bring the left arm behind the back and try to touch the right thigh. Turn the head to the left as much as possible until you feel a gentle but firm twist on the spine (you may hear small cracks of the spine being readjusted). Repeat on the other side (by bending the left leg). Try this pose five times on each side.

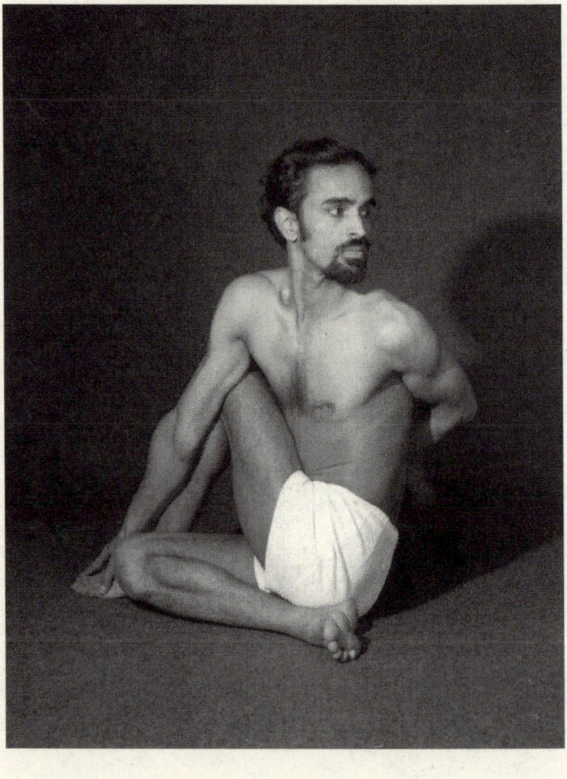

Benefits of Pose

- Helps and strengthens the legs, arms, hip joints, whole back, abdominal organs and neck
- Improves digestion and relieves many digestive complaints, including chronic constipation
- May improve functioning of the liver, spleen and pancreas
- Improves respiration and circulation in the entire body
- Because of the pressure on the artery at the base of the genitals, this pose may reduce nocturnal and involuntary emissions of semen
- Regular practice may delay or prevent the enlargement of the prostate in older males as well as tone the bladder to help normalize urine flow and frequency
- Increases flexibility in the spine and facilitates the flow of vital energy throughout the *cakras* and esoteric nervous system

Mantras

1. णमो आयरियाणं :: ṇamo āyariyāṇaṁ
2. ॐ ह्रीं श्रीं णमो आयरियाणं :: om hrīṁ śrīṁ ṇamo āyariyāṇaṁ
3. ॐ ह्रीं श्रीं अर्हं आचार्योभ्यो णमो नमः :: om hrīṁ śrīṁ arhaṁ ācāryobhyo ṇamo namaḥ
4. आयरिय णमोकारो सव्वपाव पन्नासनो :: āyariya ṇamokāro savvapāva pannāsano

Benefits of *Mantras*

- *Mantra* #2 alleviates affliction of and/or fortifies Jupiter; chanting this *mantra* with a red colour mālā also pacifies Mars
- *Mantra* #4 is useful to those who find it difficult to do *upavāsa*: reciting it 200 times (about two mālās) will give the benefit of doing one *upavāsa*
- Protection from flooding by water bodies and excessive rain
- Protection of the *sādhaka*'s person and home from fire
- Reduction of the power of enemies
- Protection of skin from excessive temperature and solar radiation
- *Ācāryas* protect the right ear

INVOCATION

गुण हैं, छत्तीस पूर, धरत धर्म उर, मारत करम क्रूर, सुमति विचारी है

अधिक मधुर वेण, कोई नहीं लोपे केण, सकल जिवों का सेण, कीरत उपारी है

ऐसे आचार्या जी को, वंदना हमारी है

guṇa hai, chattīsa pūra, dharata dharma ura, mārata karama krūra, sumati vicārī hai

adhika madhura veṇa, koī nahiṅ lope keṇa, sakala jivo kā seṇa, kīrata upārī hai

aise ācārya jī ko, vaṅdanā hamārī hai

Ācāryas have 36 great qualities. They hold religion in their heart. They avoid the four *kaśāyas* which create negative karma. They are the heads of Jaina congregations. They follow the *pañcamahāvrata* happily and guide others to follow them. They care for all living beings. Their fame has no parallel. We give our obeisance to them.

- Pratikramaṇasutra

Uvajjhāyāsana

卐

The fourth line of the *Ṇamokāra Mantra* pays homage to the *upādhyāyas*,[31] those ascetics who in addition to normal ascetic practices and preaching to the laity, additionally engage in deep study of the scriptures. Jaina *upādhyāyas* study the 11 *aṅgas*, the 12 *upaṅgas*, and specialize in teaching the Jaina *dharma* to monks and nuns. Lord Mahāvīra preached that *paḍhamaṁ ṇāṇaṁ taodayā*, meaning 'first comes knowledge, then compassion'. Knowledge is indispensable for reaching higher states of *dharma* and *sādhana*, hence the lofty position of the *upādhyāya*.

In order to successfully teach others, particularly monks and nuns, an *upādhyāya* has to be as firm, hard and powerful as a *vajra* (diamond or thunderbolt). *Vajrāsana* aptly characterizes the nature and attitude of the *upādhyāya*, and so I have termed it as *uvajjhāyāsana*.

Procedure

Kneel on a clean mat. Let the big toes of both feet touch each other with the heels spread outwards in a trough form. The knees and thighs should touch each other. Rest the buttocks on the trough of the heels. The head, neck and back should be in a

[31] *Uvajjhāya* in *ardhamāgadhī*

straight line. Breathe in and pull the shoulders backwards so that the shoulder blades are touching each other. Hold the body stiff and still for at least 10-15 seconds. Breathing out, relax the entire body. If comfortable, this position can also be held for much longer times (for example, it is an *āsana* for meditation).

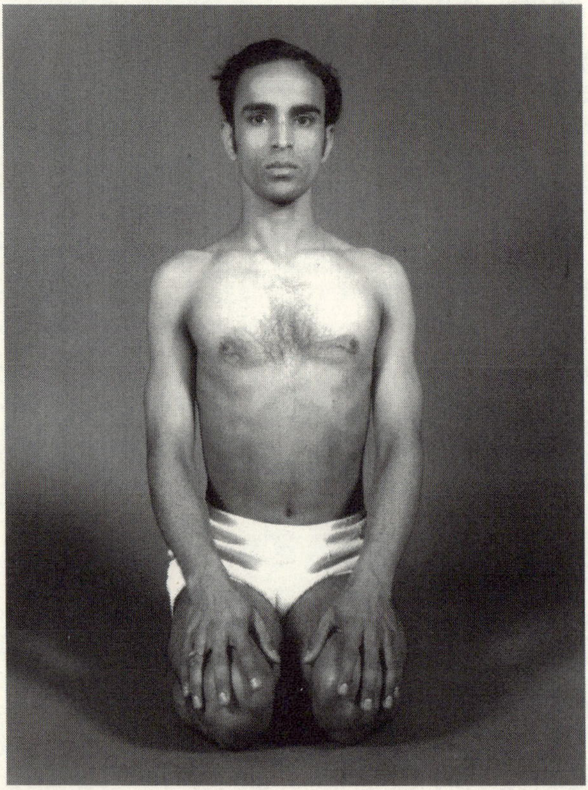

Benefits of Pose

- This pose helps the feet, knees, legs, hips and back
- Balances gases in the stomach and colon, thus aiding digestion

- Broadens the chest
- Spine becomes supple and poor pose is corrected
- Allows the practitioner to meditate for a long time
- Sitting in this pose facilitates the memory (i.e., sit in *uvajjhāyāsana* while memorizing things)

Mantras

1. णमो उवज्झायाणं :: ṇamo uvajjhāyāṇaṁ
2. ॐ ह्रीं णमो उवज्झायाणं :: om hrīṁ ṇamo uvajjhāyāṇaṁ
3. ॐ ह्रीं श्रीं अर्हं उपाध्यायोभ्यो णमो नमः :: om hrīṁ śrīṁ arhaṁ upadhyāyobhyo ṇamo namaḥ
4. ॐ ह्रां ह्रीं ह्रुं ह्रूं ह्रः अ सि आ उ सा नमः :: om hrāṁ hrīṁ hruṁ hrūṁ hraḥ a si ā u sā namaḥ
5. उवज्झाया णमोकारो सव्वपाव पन्नासनो :: uvajjhāyā ṇamokāro savvapāva pannāsano

Benefits of *Mantras*

- *Upādhyāyas* protect the heart, ear and arms
- Alleviate affliction of and/or fortify Mercury
- *Mantra* #4: chanting two *mālās* of this *mantra* everyday will help to reduce/remove *karma*s and facilitate the path to *mokṣa* in a future life

INVOCATION

पढत इग्यारे अंग, करमांसुं करे जंग, पाखंडी को मान भंग, करण हुसियारी है

चवदे पूरव धार, जानत आगम सार, भवियन के सुखकार, भ्रमता निवारी है

तप करी तावे तन, ममता निवारी है, ऐसे उपध्यायजी को, वंदना हमारी है

paḍhata igyāre aṅga, karamāṅsu kare jaṅg, pākhaṇḍī ko māna bhaṅga, karaṇa husiyārī hai

cavade purava dhāra, jānata āgama sāra, bhaviyana ke sukhakāra, bhramatā nivārī hai

tapa karī tāve tana, mamatā nivārī hai, aise upadhyāyajī ko, vaṅdanā hamārī hai

The *upādhyāyas* study the 11 *aṅgas*, 12 *upaṅgas* and the four *mūlasutras* in great depth. They successfully debate with arrogant *ekāntavādins* or divine entities. The are not *jina* or *kevali* but for us, they are like *jinas* or *kevalis*. The remove the darkness from our minds due to *mithyātva*, and they put *śrāvakas* and *śrāvikas* on the correct path. We give our obeisance to them.

- Pratikramaṇasutra

Sāhuāsana

卐卐

The person who thinks of only good things for themselves and for others is called a *sādhu*,[32] and the fifth line of the *Ṇamokāra Mantra* invokes with reverence these renunciate men and women of all faiths. True Jaina *sadhus* (male) and *sādhvis* (female) are rare humans. They have forsaken all that is commonly thought of as making life worth living: family relationships, physical relationships, wealth, fame, power, comfort, pleasures and luxuries of all kinds. They engage in strict adherence to *ahiṁsa* and the other *mahāvratas* of Jainism, abjuring violence to all living beings and even going so far as to attempt to protect elemental bodies (air, fire, water, earth). They are constantly engaged in the pursuit of self-realization.

These *sādhus* and *sādhvis* serve as a bridge between humanity and the latent power and glory of the Soul. Seeing these ordinary humans living an extraordinary lifestyle makes us believe that we too can cross the bridge across the ocean of suffering, the bridge created by the Tīrthaṅkaras. Therefore, I have renamed Haṭha Yoga's *setubandhāsana* (bridge pose) as *sāhuāsana*.

[32] *Sāhu* in *ardhamāgadhī*

Procedure

Lie face up on a clean mat. The arms should be on the floor in line with the torso. Bend both legs so that the heels touch the buttocks. Hold the ankles with both hands. If you cannot hold the heels, place the palms next to the ankles on the floor. Breathe in deeply and raise the buttocks, arching the back so that the chest touches the chin. The shoulders, neck and head should rest on the floor and the body should be in the shape of an bridge sloping upwards. Hold the pose for as long as you can retain the breath (try for at least 10-15 seconds). Breathing out, lower the buttocks slowly an inch at a time, eventually resting the body completely on the floor. Practice this pose 3-4 times. You can also stay in this pose for an extended length of time, breathing in and out slowly.

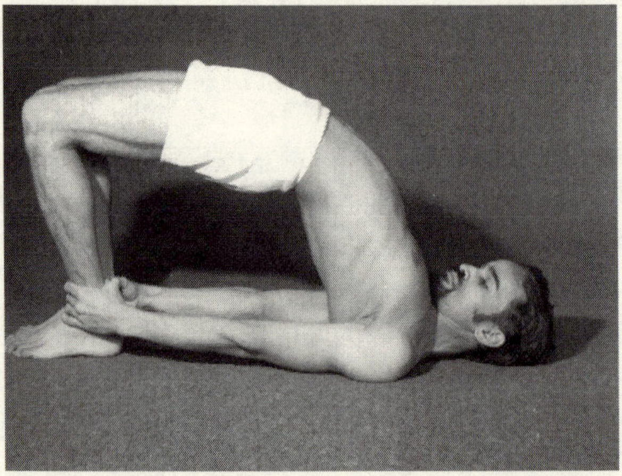

Benefits of Pose

- A primary benefit of this pose is that it helps you breathe correctly; that is, breathing through the diaphragm/ abdomen rather than incorrectly from the chest
- May realign displaced internal organs (intestines, colon, etc.) thereby reducing the prospect of disease and pain
- Tones the calves, thighs & buttocks
- Makes the entire body flexible and strong
- Reduces menstrual pain
- Reduces hip and back pain
- Improves thyroid function
- May help alleviate symptoms of asthma

Mantras

1. णमो लोए सव्व साहुणं :: ṇamo loe savva sāhuṇaṁ
2. ॐ ह्रीं णमो लोए सव्व साहुणं :: om hrīṁ ṇamo loe savva sāhuṇaṁ
3. ॐ ऐं ह्रीं णमो लोए सव्व साहुणं :: om aīṁ hrīṁ ṇamo loe savva sāhuṇaṁ
4. ॐ ह्रीं श्रीं अर्हं गौतम प्रमुख सर्व साधुभ्यो णमो नमः :: om hrīṁ śrīṁ arhaṁ gautama pramukha sarva sādhubhyo ṇamo namaḥ
5. ॐ ह्रीं अर्हं अ सि आ उ सा क्लीं नमः :: om hrīṁ arhaṁ a si ā u sā klīṁ namaḥ

Benefits of *Mantras*

- Alleviate affliction of and/or fortify Saturn, Rāhu, Ketu

- Remove enemies and enmity
- *Mantra* #5 removes mental and physical poison
- *Sādhus* protect both feet

INVOCATION

आदरी संयम भार, करणी करे अपार, समिति गुपति धार, विकथा निवारी है

जयणा करे छः काय, सावद्य न बोले वाय, बुझाय कषाय लाय,

किरिया भंडारी है

कहत है तिलोकरिख, करमां को टाले विष, ऐसे मुनिराजजी को, वंदना हमारी है

ādarī saṁyama bhāra, karaṇī kare apāra, samati gupati dhāra, vikathā nivārī hai

jayaṇā kare chaḥ kaya, sāvadya na bole vāya, bujhāya kaṣāya lāya, kiriyā bhaṅḍārī hai

kahata hai tilokarīkha, karamāṅ ko ṭāle viṣa, aise munirājajī ko, vaṅdanā hamārī hai

Sādhus and *sādhvis* have 27 good qualities. They follow the five *ācāra*, protect six *kāya* living beings, avoid seven vices, conquer eight types of ego, follow 10-fold *yati dharma*, avoid 18 *pāpasthānas*, win over 22 *pariṣayas*, avoid 33 *āśātanās*, and avoid 42 faults of *gocarī*. They do not partake of food and drinks that are *sachitta*, only those that are *achitta*. They pull out their hair regularly and walk barefoot. We give our obeisance to them.

- Pratikramaṇasutra

Appendix 1

Āsana & Ānupūrvī

Here is a simple way to integrate the last five given Jaina *āsanas* and *mantra* for daily practice. *Ānupūrvī* is a type of Jaina *yantra* using the numbers 1-2-3-4-5 in different arrangements. Utilizing the *ānupūrvī* can help the *sādhaka* achieve concentration and clarity as well as sharpen the memory.

One portion of an *ānupūrvī* is given below:

1	2	3	4	5
3	4	5	1	2
5	1	2	3	4
2	3	4	5	1
4	5	1	2	3

- When you see the number 1 – perform *arihaṁtāsana* as you recite *ṇamo arihaṁtānaṁ.*
- When you see the number 2 – perform *siddhāsana* as you recite *ṇamo siddhānaṁ.*

- When you see the number 3 – perform *āyariāsana* as you recite *ṇamo āyariānaṁ.*
- When you see the number 4 – perform *uvajjhāyasana* as you recite *ṇamo uvajjhāyānaṁ.*
- When you see the number 5 – perform *sāhuāsana* as you recite *ṇamo loe savva sāhunaṁ.*

Completing the entire *ānupūrvī* at once may be strenuous. The *sādhaka* may start with the first line of the *ānupūrvī*, and then as stamina increases, add additional lines until he/she is able to complete the entire *ānupūrvī*, and then, as time and ability permit, go beyond one *ānupūrvī*. The standard Jaina *ānupūrvī* is made up of 24 tables and is widely available.

Appendix 2

Health Guidelines from the *Sthānāṅgasūtra*

Nine Causes of Illness

1. Excessive eating and sitting
2. Eating when one has indigestion, or eating improper food and sitting a wrong posture
3. Sleeping too much
4. Not sleeping enough or forcefully staying awake
5. Not moving bowels or restricting bowel movements
6. Holding in the urine for an excessive time
7. Excessive walking or running
8. Eating improper food (wrong combinations; stale, spoiled, highly processed or rotten food)
9. Overusing the five senses and excessive sexual activity

Recommendations for Eating

1. While eating, keep the mind focused on the act of eating
2. Do not eat in a hurry or too fast
3. Do not eat too slowly or linger too long at the table
4. Do not talk or laugh while eating

ॐ

EXERCISE ~ BREATHE ~ LOVE ~ MEDITATE ~ REALIZE

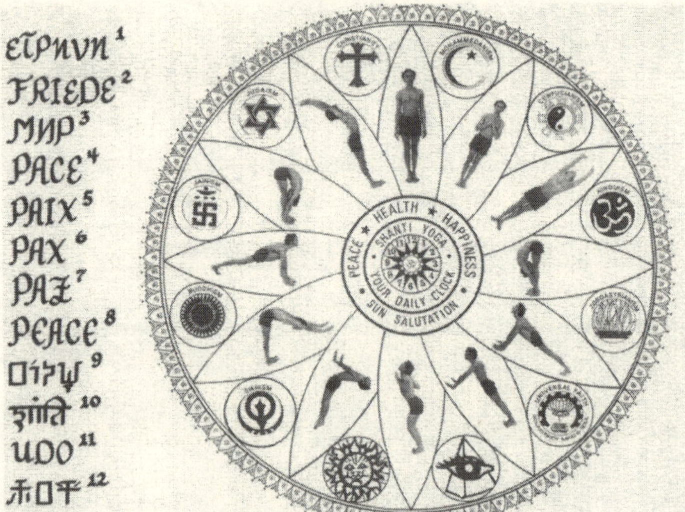

Surya Namaskāra – Sun Salutation

Bibliography

Amar Muni, Upādhyāya. Mahāmantra Navakāra. Agra: Sanmati Jñānapiṭha, 1981.

Amar Muni, Upādhyāya. Yoga Śāstra Eka Pariśīlana. Agra: Sanmati Jñānapiṭha, 1963.

Amolakṛṣi, Ācārya. Jain Tattva Prakaśa. Dhulia: Śrī Amol Jain Jñānalaya, 1968.

Amolakṛṣi, Ācārya. Dhyan-Kalpataru. Dhulia: Śrī Amol Jain Jñānalaya, 1957.

Ātmārāmji, Upādhyāya. Jaināgamo me Aṣṭānga Yoga. Zira, Ferozepur.

Chapple, Christopher Key, ed. Yoga in Jainism. London: Routledge, 2016.

Danaos, Kosta. Nei Kung. Rochester, VT: Inner Traditions, 2002.

Devendramuni, Ācārya. Jaina Religion and Philosophy. Udaipur: Tāraka Guru Jaina Granthālaya, 1985.

Kuṇḍakuṇḍa Vijayji. Namaskāra Cintāmaṇī. Ajmer: Śrī Jinadattasuri Manḍal, 1974.

Kevalamuni, Upādhyāya. Sacitra Ṇamokāramahāmantra. Agra: Divākar Publications, 1991.

Goyal, Devendra K, tr. The Path to Enlightenment, Svayambhu Stotra by Samantabhadra. New Delhi: Radiant Publishers, 2000.

Jinkīrti Suri Mahārāja, Śrī. Śrī-mantra-rajā-guṇa-kalpamahodadhi. Bikāner: 1920.

Nagar, Shanti Lal. Glory of Jaina Tīrthaṅkaras. Delhi: Eastern Book Linkers, 2006.

Quarnstrom, Olle. The Yogaśāstra of Hemacandra. Cambridge: Harvard University Press, 2002.

Rajendra, Muni. Cauvisa Tīrthaṅkāra. Udaipur: Tāraka Guru Jaina Granthālaya, 1976.

Samadarśi, Muni, ed. Yoga Śāstra Ācārya Hemacandra. Agra: 1963.

Yaśā, Sādhvī Śrī, ed. Savidhi Sacitra Pratikramaṇa Sutra. Nāsika: 1993.

Praise for the First Edition

Shantilal Parakh is a promising young man. He wishes to give the big picture of Jainism to the whole world. He is making great efforts to spread the teachings and message of Lord Mahāvīra to many soul-searching minds. In this regard, he has used the 24 *lānchans* of the Tīrthaṅkaras to create yogic poses to help improve the physical and mental health of Jain *śrāvakas* and *śrāvikas*. May his efforts be successful around the world. These are my good wishes for him.

- ***Mālava Keśari Saubhāgyamalji Mahārāja***

It is great news that your book *Tīrthaṅkarāsana* is being published in the holy presence of Ācāryasamrāṭa Ānand Ṛṣi Mahārāja. His lotus hands have touched and blessed this book. I have no doubt that this book will be very helpful for people who are interested in the different forms and schools of yoga. In reality, this type of book was much needed in Jain literature. Your efforts in writing this book is praiseworthy.

I have witnessed your excellent *āsanas* at Yogaville-Utica, which was started and established by Muniśrī Suśīla Kumarji in America. I can say with confidence that the photos of the *āsanas* are literally communicating with those who see them. Your pen has given the photographs a beautiful flow. This book not only increases people's knowledge of Jain Yoga but this book will be a rock-solid monument for future generations.

My blessings for all success in this endeavour.

- ***Subhāgamuniji, Guru-brother of Ācārya Suśīla Muniji***

In Indian meditative disciplines, positive physical health is a prerequisite for deeper self-realization. Whosoever is physically unwell cannot sit steadily for longer periods. Without being able to sit steadily, one cannot meditate. And without meditation, there can be no final liberation. For this reason, there is a strong emphasis on stable and blissful *āsanas* in the eight-fold path of yoga propounded by Patañjali.

In this book on Jain Yoga, some poses are totally new while others have been dealt with in other works on yoga. The poses are named both traditionally and with the names of the Tīrthaṅkaras. For each *āsana*, *mantras* are given to deepen the engagement with the poses on the physical, mental and spiritual levels.

This purpose of this book is not only to show the proper procedures of doing the poses, but also to spread light on *dhyāna*, *mantra*, and *japa* and also to remember the kindness and grace showered upon us by great saints and *svāmis*. The writer is an accomplished meditator. The insights and essences he realized during many years of meditation have been published for the benefit of fortunate readers. The benefits of this book will be self-evident as you delve deeper into yogic practices.

Sins, wickedness, bad behaviour and corruption originate in timidity caused by weak minds and weak bodies. Cowardly man, in order to fulfil his desires, chooses questionable means. If people become physically and mentally fit through yoga and meditation, all bad elements of society will be reduced. This book will help you to become physically and mentally super strong.

- ***Pravin Ṛṣiji Mahārāja***

About the Author

Shanti is an internationally known Yoga teacher, Reflexologist, Metaphysician and Healer. He served for many years as the Vice-Chair of the International Mahavir Jain Mission, having been appointed directly by the Chair and Founder, Ācārya Suśila Kumarji.

Even though Shanti was educated in the sciences from the Indian Institute of Technology (IIT), he has been practicing yoga for over 50 years and has been reading palms and working on the hands and feet for over 45 years. Shanti has won championships in Haṭha yoga (including with the Maharashtra State Gymnastic Association) and has taught at Brock University, the State University of New York at Buffalo (four-credit course in yoga and two-credit course in Jainism), Buffalo State College, Niagara University and other colleges in the Buffalo area. Shanti is a certified reflexologist and is a member of the Ontario College of Reflexology and the Federation of Ontario Yoga Teachers. He also teaches advanced reflexology to reflexologists and advanced yoga to yoga teachers.

Shanti has appeared on television programs in the Niagara Region, Toronto and Western New York. There have been articles about Shanti in major newspapers across the USA, Canada and India. He has published books and posters on yoga and reflexology. Shanti has lectured on and demonstrated yoga at international conferences in India, Canada and the USA. In the late 1980s, he completed a peace and goodwill mission to Poland, Hungary, Czechoslovakia, East Germany, and the Soviet Union with Ācārya Suśila Kumarji, and has taken groups to India. Shanti holds an M.A. from the State University of New York at Buffalo and an M.Sc. from the Indian Institute of Technology (Mumbai) where he was a silver medallist.

For further inquiries, you may contact the author directly:

Tel.: +1-905-374-3067
Email: shasum108@yahoo.ca
Website: www.shanti-yoga.ca

About the Editor

Dinesh S. Parakh is a lawyer and former official with the United Nations. He holds a B.A. from Yale University and an M.A. & J.D. from the University of Toronto. Since he was a teenager, Dinesh has had a deep and abiding interest in Indian esoterica (including yoga, *taṅtra*, Sanskrit & *jyotiṣa*). He has been studying *jyotiṣa* with renowned *jyotiṣa* master Śrī Hart deFouw since 2005, and is also a long-term practitioner of Okinawan *gōjū-ryū* karate.